THE KIDDUSH CUP

Also by Yaffa Liebermann

Physical Therapist, APTA Geriatric Certified Specialist

Stroke Restoration - Functional Movement for Patients and Caregivers

I Stand Up Straight: Poem and Exercises

Rachel, Pedro and Friends Stand Up Straight Activity Book

Rachel, Pedro and Friends Sit Up Straight Activity Book

THE KIDDUSH CUP

The Story of Rachel Lajzerowicz and Her Aliyah
From Zdunska Wola, Poland to Israel in 1939

Written by Rachel's daughter
Yaffa Liebermann

Illustrated by
Katie Sokolowski

Edited by Rachel's granddaughter **Tamar Liebermann Brooks**
and great granddaughters, **Kaila Brooks, and Rachel Brooks**

First edition 2020
Second edition 2023

ISBN 9780578827186 (hardcover)
ISBN 9780578827193 (ebook)

Cataloguing-in-Publication data for this book is available from the Library of Congress (LC Control No. number 2020925280)

Published by Posture and Breathing LLC
E mail: postureandbreathing@gmail.com
Fax (732) 493-4285

Table of Contents

INTRODUCTION

In 1939 my mother arrived in Israel as an illegal immigrant, and her story stayed with me throughout my life. I used to ask her to recount her story when we made dough for a yeast cake or when we worked in the vegetable garden picking strawberries. I drew courage from her history and her strong desire to survive. The events she went through deepened my belief in God and gave me more appreciation of our existence.

I can still recall when I sat with my parents in 1992 and asked them to share the story of their lives with me. I was inspired to document her story after a visit to Freedom Park in Arlington, Virginia on December 14, 1998. Carved bricks from the Warsaw Ghetto were placed there to remind the world of the historical uprising for freedom from April 19 to May 16, 1943. The few Jews that fought had no chance of winning against the German war monster. They died fighting. The fact that a story from Jewish history was presented as one of the few outstanding events in the fight for human freedom inspired me to share my mother's past. My daughter, Hadas, suggested we visit Poland in 2002 to better understand, see, and feel the way my mother lived. I appreciate this trip with my daughter as it shaped me forever.

As I looked deeper into my mother's past in Poland, I found that she had a good life in her village and in Lodz. Her family made a living with whatever they had in their means and did not complain. From the pictures we can see that she and her friends were dressed well in tailored clothes while in Poland. She did not have a tailored dress in Israel, and she never complained about the differences.

While writing her story I wanted to better understand why the Jewish people made others envy them and jealous of their achievement. I tried to understand why every government in Europe, Asia, and Africa wanted to kick them out of their country. I found some answers and put them in writing in this story.

The old photographs in this book are from my family archives. The photographs of antique items are from my personal antique collection.

The modern photographs of cooking, beaches and Masada are from my children's photo albums.

The beautiful illustrations were made especially for this book by Katie Sokolowski Ph.D. in neurotoxicology.

I will describe Rachel's life in Poland and the reasons that made her make an Aliyah (ascending) to Israel. I hope you will learn about the courage that these young Jewish people possessed to act in time and save themselves from the Nazi Regime. I hope you will discover the challenges of the Aliyah to Israel and the precision needed to unite every piece of the puzzle in order to bring Jews to their promised land.

Finally, I hope you enjoy the book.

LIFE IN ZDUŃSKA WOLA, POLAND - AROUND 1920

This story is about a girl named Rachel who was born to the Lajzerowicz family in 1912 in a town named Zduńska Wola near Lodz, Poland. Her parents' names were Nacha and Eliezer. They had eight children: Szymon-Binem, Mordechai-Mayer, Esther-Yetta, Rachel, Joseph, Shoshana, Luba, and Nechemia. Eventually and unfortunately, most of the family was killed in concentration camps by the Nazi Regime, but four of the siblings survived. Nechemia moved to America in 1937, while Joseph and Rachel made Aliyah to Israel, and Shoshana arrived in Israel in 1946.

Rachel had a joyful childhood. She was deeply loved by her parents and respected by her siblings and school friends. She followed her heart, trusted her instinct, and was realistic. Rachel understood the issues in Poland and made choices that saved her life. Join me on the winding path that led Rachel to Israel, the promised land. The following section describes the history of the town where she was raised.

ZDUŃSKA WOLA HISTORY FROM 1773-1938

Zduńska Wola was a district capital in the province of Lodz, Poland. From 1525 to 1679, this town was considered to be under a "feudal" system as the peasants were compelled to provide free labor to their feudal "Paritz" (translated from Polish: "estate owner"). The Paritz in the area wanted to establish a new town but he needed to obtain a royal permit that was kept from him for a long time. The King only granted permission for a new village in 1773. It was built with a marketplace that was operating only once a month. The name of the village, "Wola," indicates that the Paritz was ex-feudal (Wola means goodwill or freedom from paying taxes). It is assumed that the first name followed several "pottery" craftsmen who lived in the village and repaired ovens ("zdun" in Polish). The village continuously changed names until the middle of the 17th century when the name "Zduńska Wola" was established ([1]).

Figure 1: Old Zduńska Wola.

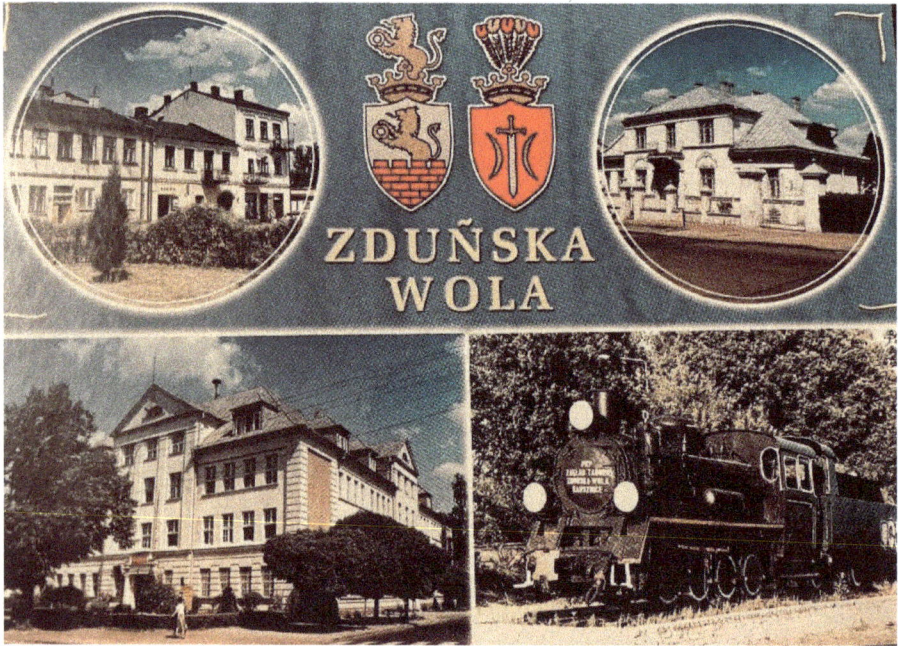
Figure 2: A postcard from Zedunska Wola 2002.

This small hamlet was the estate of a feudal middle-class family. In 1788, eleven Jewish families moved into town. Among them were four tailors, two furriers, two merchants, one baker, one barber, and one unknown worker. This increased Zduńska Wola's population from twelve peasant families to twenty-three families in total. The Jewish newcomers were instructed to build their homes on the two streets nearest to the market.

In 1825, when the village was declared a town, the mobilization and settling of the Jews did not cause any difficulties as long as they stayed within those two streets. Surrounding the Jewish settlement, aristocrats conducted a propaganda campaign with the local population to prevent the Jews from operating in public houses and breweries. As a result, Jewish people went to develop the textile industry as it was the only close area of business (2).

Zduńska Wola grew to be an important town. At the end of the eighteenth century, there were fifteen new houses in Czekai (yet to be named Zduńska Wola). A synagogue, a church, and a council house were built by the people of the village. In addition, three buildings were built by the Jewish residents and four were built by the Christians

13

residents as housing solutions for people who came to settle in town. The community had natural resources, but the timber, lime, and stone could not be transported elsewhere due to the lack of a river. Therefore, they built houses that brought satisfactory rent for the Paritz. In the year 1825, his efforts bore fruit, and this consolidated area was recognized as the industrial town of Zduńska Wola. Strangely, after gaining municipal status, the relationship between Jews and Christians changed.

The Jewish population grew rapidly, but their conditions were unfavorable. They were denied many rights and various unreasonable restrictions were imposed. The town municipal and the central authorities demanded that Jewish immigration buildings in the town be limited. They declared that no local Jewish settler should be in possession of a license for a public house and they were interested in hindering additional settlement of Jews.

Meanwhile, many merchants came from neighboring countries to trade, and there was a vital need to establish a public house. The limited rights regarding the dwelling places of Jews lasted five years. At the beginning of 1830, the poor Jews started to settle in other parts of the town. Because many of them did not have the resources to build brick houses, they built wooden ones, whereupon the local authorities intervened, renewed restrictions, and even augmented them. Jews were pushed out of their houses and directed back to the original two streets.

People are always looking for a good source of income to provide for their family. The German and Polish people heard of the developing town and moved into the area as they were skilled in processing and manufacturing textile. The census in 1931 showed that of the 22,425 people who lived in Zduńska Wola about 35% were Jewish, 25% were German, and 40% were Polish.

In 1853, Christian settlers complained to the regional court representative that "Jews are spreading all over town contrary to the restrictions imposed in 1848, and based on a license from the district commissioner, are putting up *huts*" (in the document, the term 'hut' is stressed). From that moment onwards it was decided that every Jew who attempted to build in the prohibited streets was required to prove that they were complying with the terms demanded previously (3).

The position, rights, and conditions granted to Jews in Zduńska Wola were like those in Lodz and Zagers. The same applied to the number of Jews with "special rights." One paragraph stated, "In Zduńska Wola, Jews will be permitted to live in other streets with the condition that they build on empty lots or build brick houses covered in tiled roofs to replace wooden houses. They must also be industrialists or independent artisans and manage their own weaving workshops. The same applies to major textile merchants." This arrangement was only available to the Jewish population who could afford it, to encourage investment in building and expanding the town.

An example of the discrimination against Jews is as follows: "In 1862, Zelig Herschfinkel of Warsaw bought a wooden house with the purpose of demolishing it and putting up a brick house instead. He applied for a license and wrote:

1. I know how to read and write in Polish.

2. I send my children to a Polish school, and they know both the Polish and German languages fluently. They also read and write in both.

3. My family and I, do not wear traditional Jewish clothes and our clothes are not different from other "cultured" people.

4. As custodian of treasury income of the town, a lottery agent, and a wholesale wood dealer, I openly manage the turnover of three enterprises. I have my own capital amounting to the sum of 3,000 ruble (cash)" (3).

If this man was not Jewish, he probably would not have to prove his income.

As the years continued, the Jewish population grew. In 1893, the small synagogue was replaced with a larger one and it stood strong until the Second World War. The first institute for modern education, the Talmud school was founded in ZW at the end of the 19th century. The students attended the school rather than gather in one of the homes and a teacher (Melamed) would come to teach them.

After World War I, Zduńska Wola rapidly regained its economic status. The Jews of the town earned their livelihoods primarily from commerce and most of the jobs connected to the textile industry. In the 1930s, seventy textile factories were owned by Jews, most of them were of average size but a few were large and had 1,100 workers, approximately half of whom were Jewish. Nearly 360 workshops were owned by Jews, and they specialized in various crafts such as garment manufacturing, food processing, metal, leather products, and construction. These workshops employed 848 people, almost all of whom were Jewish.

The economic crisis of the 1930s hurt Zduńska Wola's factories less than it did the larger factories in the region. The lower wages in Zduńska Wola (about 80% of the average wage in Lodz) and the ability of smaller factories, most of which were home-based, contributed to this phenomenon and helped the village adapt to the difficult circumstances.

Around that time, the Jewish/Israeli organizations grew: Agudat Yisra'el (The Association of Israel) was active in all aspects of Torah/Bible culture and rituals. Other active organizations included The Zionists and Mizrachi party ("Easterner", a religious Zionist party). Then in 1927, a women's organization was established called "Bnot Agudat Yisra'el" (Daughters of Israel) (4)(5).

In 1929, more establishments were founded. A branch of HeChalutz ("The Israeli Pioneer") set up a local training farm using the money that they had earned from baking and selling matzah (unleavened bread). Bikur Cholim Society helped sick people. The largest bank in Zduńska Wola established "Tomchei Aniyim" (Supporters of the Poor), "Beit Lechem" (House of Bread), and the Society for the Promotion of Handicrafts.

In the 1930s, in addition to the Talmud Torah, the Jewish community founded Yesodei HaTorah for boys and Bet Yakov for the girls. It was a town with Jewish, Polish, and German descendants. There were Polish public schools for everyone and Jewish schools that were private.

The Jewish school curriculum had extracurriculars in addition to the basic studies: like drama and singing classes.

There was time to be focused on learning and time to rejoice and dance. The students were serious in their studies, they attended school and did their homework, but when there was a Simcha (happiness) they celebrated the occasion.

In a Bar Mitzvah, the main event was the boy that reached 13 years of age reading from the Tora and reciting the prayers. To celebrate this turning point in his life, from a child to a man, and make it happy occasion and memorable, the friends and family danced around and with him. In a wedding, the participants celebrated by dancing in front of the newlyweds or dancing separately with the groom and the bride. Singing was part of life. On Friday night dinner, after the meal, it was the time to sing.

The prayers in the synagogue were a combination of silence, recitation and song. This is the reason the extracurriculars were important to prepare for life in the community.

In the center of the town was the marketplace, "Rynek," which was a square surrounded by apartment houses. A regular building had two- or three-story houses. Traditionally, the first floor was a store, and the second and third floors were living quarters for the owners or tenants.

This was the village where the Lajzerowicz family grew.

THE LIVES OF THE LAJZEROWICZ FAMILY IN THE COMMUNITY

The Lajzerowicz family lived close to the market in the area designated to Jews. Most of the Jews in Zduńska Wola were Orthodox, and most Christians were Catholics. The Jews had to follow two authorities: the Polish government (global and local) and the Jewish organization that was made of elected officials.

Figure 3: Nacha with her grandparents (circa 1880).

Figure 4: Yaffa in front of the Zdunska Wola cemetery memorial plaque (2002) - where the Lajzerowicz family is buried.

Figure 5: The Lajzerowicz family minus two boys - Joseph is in Israel. Rachel is standing in the upper row (1934).

Figure 6: Nechemia, who went to America (1937).

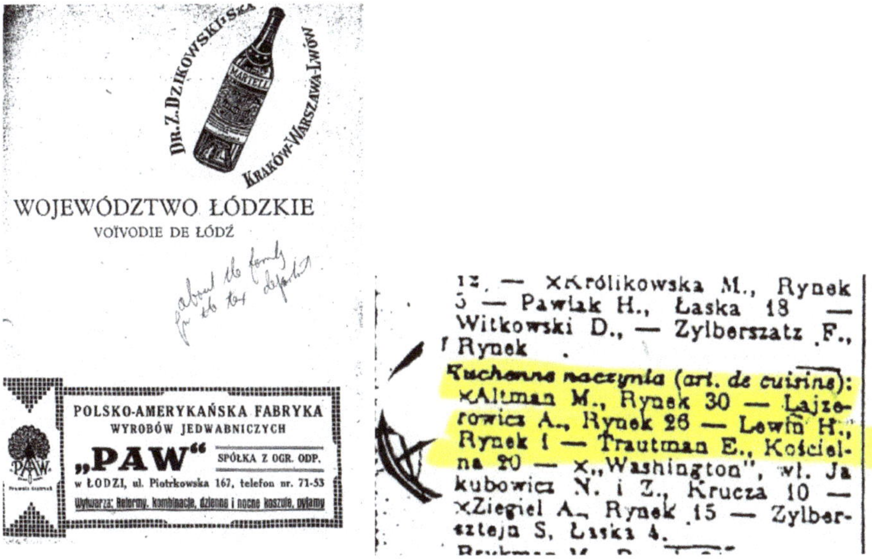

Figure 7: Lajzerowicz residency in Zduńska Wola (1934) and notes from the Lodz city documentation.

The Rabbi was the head of the community. The criteria to be chosen for this position is an appreciation for humankind, wisdom, and a deep understanding of Biblical studies. He was also the judge, counselor, and supporter. He was the head of the Jewish school, the "Yeshiva" that its official language was Yiddish.

The Jewish community was a tight knit group. It consisted of scholars and workers, who together raised children, celebrated births, Bar-Mitzvahs, weddings, and supported each other at sad times (6).

Figure 8: Boys studying in the Chader.

Figure 9: Yaffa in front of a synagogue in Warsaw (2002).

The Jewish community focused on education and made sure everyone had the opportunity to study. Synagogue was for all ages: toddlers up to adults. The "Chader" was the kindergarten school, and grade school was for ages six and older. The boys went to a Yeshiva, and the girls studied in "Bnot Ya'akov." Working people had evening Bible study sessions. The schools were attached to the beautiful synagogue which had windows and towers that stood tall and proud. The arc in the synagogue was a wooden door with figures carved from wood. On top of the arc, was an engraving of the Ten Commandments in white stone. Above the Ten Commandments, was the Star of David, the symbol of Judaism.

22

Figure 10: Rachel going to a girl's school in the synagogue.

Figure 11: Inside a synagogue in Warsaw (2002).

Rachel attended public school in the morning and in the afternoon she switched to a Jewish school. The girls ran from school to school with their books and notebooks. Rachel enjoyed studying; she strived to be a good student and pressured herself to succeed. Rachel was an attentive student, listened to instructions and followed them. She always finished her homework on time and never missed a day of school. The teachers recognized her unique devotion to education, and they honored Rachel for her dedication with a certificate for perfect attendance.

The girls had fun running during summer sometimes using a scooter, sliding in the snow during winter, and most of all jumping into puddles of mud and dirt. Their feet froze, but who cared? They were young and life was at its best.

Figure 12: A scooter kids would ride while playing

One summer day, mother Nacha, father Eliezer, Szymon-Binem, and Mordechai-Mayer were not around; they went to listen to the Rabbi giving "Dvar-Torah" (a Biblical study). Meanwhile, Rachel and a few kids played hide and seek. They dashed in and out of the house, their faces flashed with red color and their shirts wet from sweat as the weather was very hot. Eventually, they got a little hungry and thirsty.

Rachel remembered the place in the attic where the family stored apples for the winter. Being the caring and loving girl that she was, Rachel climbed up the ladder, found the right basket, and threw the apples one by one down to the children. Each child cheered loudly when they caught the juicy apple and ate it with pleasure. Rachel smiled when she heard their cheers. Some children had a little juice running down their chin, but as their hungry bellies became satisfied, their faces became relaxed. The evening came, and they all went home with bright smiles.

Later, Rachel's mother discovered the missing basket, understood the circumstances of its disappearance, and forgave Rachel. But somehow, Rachel did not forgive herself because she had taken food from her own family, which they stored specifically for the approaching days. She remembered the act as the most unacceptable event in her childhood, yet she still smiled at the memories of the happy children.

Figure 13: Rachel throws apples to her friends.

"Parnasa" - Making a Living

It was difficult to make a living in the town and families had to work very hard to provide bread for the table and clothes to wear. Father, Mother, and the children all had responsibilities to share the heavy load of feeding a family. Father Eliezer would wake up in the morning, quietly say the morning prayer, put on his heavy boots, throw on his coat, and march into the cold breezy air. Rachel woke up early to help with the morning preparation after her father left the house.

Rachel prayed, "God, oh God, can you please glance toward our direction? Can you make sure that my father will come back with some good sheep's wool, so we can spin it and weave it? That we will be able to have a good meal and clothing for Rosh Hashanah (the Jewish New Year)."

Eliezer used to walk from farm to farm on hot and cold days to see if he could buy raw wool. He hiked through villages on dirt roads. When it poured heavy rain and a wagon pulled by horses passed it would spray him with mud. There were no buses, cars, or paved roads, but he had two strong feet, a caring warm heart, and a mission to provide a decent life for his family.

Rachel waited somedays impatiently for the end of the day, looking out at the corner of the Rynek to see if her father came back. As the sun set, red and yellow colors coated the sky, and the figure of a man appeared on the horizon.

"God, please God, make this shadow be him. I promise to be a good girl, just bring my father back with a full sack of wool if possible."

With a slow, steady pace, the figure grew bigger. The silhouette came closer, and it was he, her beloved father. He was tired and bent down but had a sweet smile for Rachel. He was carrying a big bag of wool.

"Thank you, God, thank you. You did your share, I will do mine," said Rachel silently while looking up to the sky.

Rachel walked back home with her father, her little hand resting in his big hand.

She said to him, "Father, I am so glad to see you. We have warm food waiting for you on the stove. Did you walk far today? Were the farmers nice to you? What kind of wool did you bring?"

"Slowly, slowly my child, one question at a time," Father replied, "I was lucky to catch a ride with Yosale's wagon today and enter a farm where they had just cut the wool." When they arrived home, Father greeted the family, hugged his wife and children, and ate his warm meal while the older children sat on the floor and prepared the wool for spinning.

Figure 14: Rachel's father returns with a sack of wool.

Taking Care of the Wool

The wool had medium thickness. The fibers were about 6 inches long and some were wavy. Rachel and Szymon-Binem washed the wool very carefully. It relaxed in the water and became fluffy, soft, and shiny. Slowly, the water changed from clear to a greasy gray from the wool. They pulled it out of the water with their fingers wide and laid it on a rack to dry. This was a very serious task: no squeezing or twisting was allowed. The following day, the wool was dry, and the spinning began. Rachel sat by the "Great Wheel" and drew the fibers out of the bundle. She attached it to the spindle, pulled it over the wheel, put her foot on the peddle, and maintained a steady and slow speed. Rachel held the wool in her hands, between her thumb and first finger, and controlled the pull. There was a precise balance between using the correct amount of fiber, treadling the foot at the appropriate speed, and adjusting the tension on the wheel.

When the fibers are spun with a subtle twist, they make a soft yarn for a sweater or clothing fabric, but if the twist was firmer, they were better suited for furnishing fabrics (7, 8, 9, 10, 11).

"Mother, please come quickly," Rachel panicked, "something got stuck." Nacha came and untangled the yarn, making sure everything was done correctly. At the end of the day, she was proud of Rachel. There were a lot of spun wool ready for Father to sale to the factory so they can process it into clothes and other fabrics and he would have money to feed his family.

Figure 15: Rachel is weaving the wool.

ZDUŃSKA WOLA OPEN MARKET

Zduńska Wola held an open market twice a week after they became a town. Rachel loved these days because it was a lot of work, but also a lot of fun. Mother Nacha and her daughters had their designated area in the market. People walked from booth to booth looking, touching, and smelling the produce. Before buying a jacket, they held up the garment to inspected for holes. Some vendors did not have a table, and they put their goods on a sheet that was laid on the ground. The buyers and sellers seemed to enjoy the day: children ran around laughing and playing while their parents bought bread, vegetables, fruit, milk products and meat, as well as tools to use at home.

Figure 16: Items found at the market. Top: A scale that uses weights to provide accurate measurements. Bottom, left: A bent straw rug beater used to beat the dust out of mattresses and rugs. Bottom, right: A primus stove to heat water used to wash beddings.

GETTING READY FOR THE MARKET DAY

PREPARING THE MILK

Nacha, Joseph, and Rachel prepared the milk products. They bought milk from the farmers around town. On their way home from the farm, they would stick their finger in the milk and lick the top of the heavy cream before they arrived home. They homogenized it by breaking the butter fat that was on the top and mixing it with the rest of the milk. Then, they pasteurized the milk. This was Joseph's job who lifted the heavy jars onto the stove and made sure the fire was strong enough to kill any bacteria that lived in it. Finally, he put all the pasteurized milk in big jars and stored them in a cool place, ready for the market day (12, 13).

MAKING THE "TWAROG" - FARMER'S CHEESE

For market day, Mother prepared the farmer's cheese ("twarog"). While she warmed the milk, she had to constantly stir it to avoid scorching. Then she turned off the heat and added buttermilk and vinegar, stirring it until the warm milk separated into fibrous curd and a green liquid. She poured that into a colander lined with cheesecloth. The fun part was tying the four corners of the cheesecloth into a knot then hanging the bag of curds to drain over the sink for about an hour, until they stopped dripping. At the end, Mother added salt and moved the cheese into a bowl that was placed by the milk in the cool basement waiting ready for the market day (14, 15, 16).

MAKING THE BUTTER

They made butter every two to three days. First, Nacha would collect the cream from the previous days. Then she skimmed its top, gathered it into a container, and placed it in the cellar. When there was enough to make a batch of butter, Rachel and Esther-Yetta took turns churning it. The churn was a stoneware jar with a large mouth that had a wooden lid and a dasher. It took about half an hour to push the dasher and lift it up and down until the thick milk transformed to butter. The two sisters used this time to practice mathematics: addition, subtraction, multiplication, and division. The time spent churning the butter depended on the temperature.

The correct temperature was the key to success. Nacha used to say, "If the cream is hot, the butter would be soft and fluffy, and it would take hours to make. If the cream is too cold, the butter forms little balls and does not stick together."

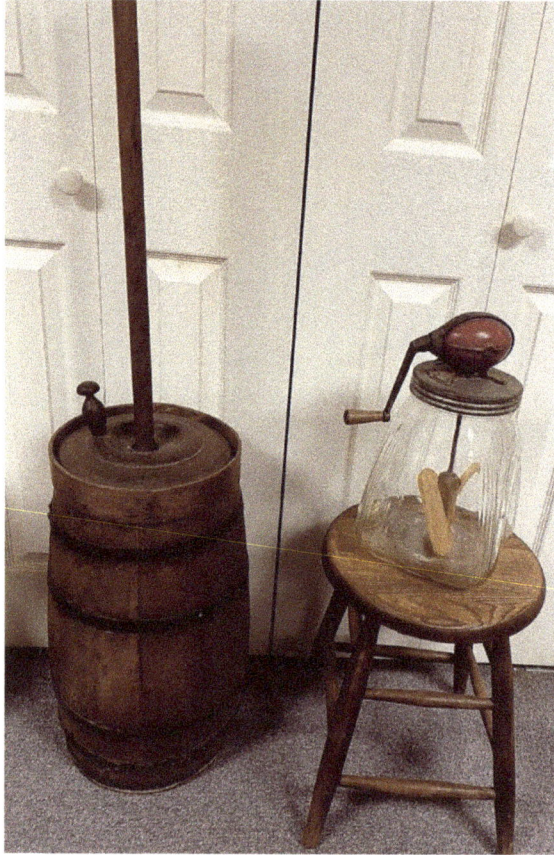

Figure 17: A standing (left) and table-top (right) butter churn.

Mother was always available to guide them. When the butter seemed ready, they rinsed it with cold water and made sure the water worked itself away. The last step, like the cheese, was to pour it into molds. This time, Rachel and Esther made sure to squeeze the butter firmly into the mold and leave no bubbles. They laid it in a pan of cold water and covered it with a cloth to cool. The left-over milk in the churn was good buttermilk used for cooking, baking, or just simple drinking. Then, they placed the butter and the buttermilk in the cellar, ready for the market day (17, 18, 19).

The market day went well; the booth had a fair number of visitors. People brought small milk containers with them, and Nacha poured into them. Women dressed in a variety of styles from elegant and colorful clothing to dresses that simply looked like rags.

Rachel observed them and quietly told her mother, "Thank God we work hard and are able to have decent clothes, food to eat, and education. Let's try to help these people who cannot help themselves."

Figure 18: Hand containers for carrying milk on the market day.

When the sun set slowly and the milk products disappeared, Nacha said, "It was a good day today, thank God. Thank you, children, for helping me so much. Now let us go home and have a good dinner with bread, butter, cheese, and milk. It is the milk that gives strength to your bones and muscles. It has so much protein and calcium. That's what you need to grow tall and strong."

With this meaningful statement, they gathered their jars as well as the new chicken and fish and went home to have a dinner with the family. They washed their hands and face and brushed their teeth. Rachel sat to do her school assignments, helped Mother prepare her little brothers and sisters for a good night's sleep, and sang "Adon Olam" ("Lord of the World") followed by "Shema Israel: Adonai Eloheinu, Adonai Echad" ("Hear, O Israel: The Lord our God, the Lord is One"). With that peaceful prayer, the children went to sleep.

Figure 19: Rachel watches her mother working in their booth.

Friday Night and Shabbat "Kodesh" (Holy Shabbat)

The family worked very hard the entire week, but, during Shabbat, they prayed, ate their best food, sang, and rested. It was believed that the seventh day was for the people to make a holy day. Shabbat made the people thank God for all they had. Everyone took time to ask for what was needed, let go of the past week, generate strength, and regroup for the next week. In the Jewish tradition, no work like driving, writing, or cooking should be done on the holy day of Shabbat. The family gathered and spent a nice time together.

"Tzedakah"

"Tzedakah" in Hebrew means giving to the poor. Mother held a special charity ritual every Friday before Sabbath, she put a few Zlotys in a small box for poor people.

Mother always said, "God has blessed us with the ability to work. We have little, but we manage. It does not matter how poor we are, there are others who cannot work and are poorer than us. So we must take care of our community. If we do not care, who will?"

Food Preparation

Figure 20: A large wick burner with two flames (left). A deconstructed two-wick burner (right).

Starting a fire was considered work, so cooking was not allowed for 24 hours beginning at sundown on Friday until sundown Saturday night, when three stars appear in the sky. The rules of the tradition allowed warming prepared food on an already warmed surface but not preparing and cooking the food. They boiled water on Friday late afternoon and placed the kettle on the wood stove ready to be used during Sabbat. Cooking or heating food was done on a wick burner (as shown in Figure 20) or on a wood stove.

Nacha and Eliezer used to say, "Everything in life that is important and meaningful needs to be planned and ready ahead of time. A day cannot be successful or good without proper preparation."

The Friday dinner preparation began at the marketplace on Thursday when Nacha bought chicken, fish, yeast, and flour. Rachel prepared the chicken for cooking a little later.

KOSHER FOOD

There were certain rules that Jews had to follow in order to be kosher, and Esther was very familiar with these restrictions. She knew that kosher food was divided into three categories: meat, dairy, and pareve. It required total separation of the meat and dairy products; they were not to be cooked or eaten together and there was a certain waiting time between eating a meat and dairy meal. The kitchen had designated areas to prepare meals from the two categories. They had separate sets of dishes, utensils, cookware, and they rinsed them separately. The pareve, was composed of foods which are neither meat nor dairy like fish, vegetable, fruit and can be eaten with meat or dairy (20, 21).

CHICKEN SOUP

Rachel took the chicken to the "Shochet," a man who ended the chicken's life with a quick cut to the throat while praying that it died without suffering. She then sat on a little bench to pluck out the feathers. Afterwards, she took it to an open fire nearby to burn the tiny feathers and then pull their left over roots out of the skin with a sharp knife. She did this so the feathers would not float in the clear soup when the poultry was cooked. The next steps were to cut it into pieces, cover it with salt on seven sides, and let it rest for one hour. Then she rinsed it and let it sit in water for half an hour. All of this was done to make the chicken kosher, cooked without blood, following the rules of the kosher law.

To make chicken soup, Mother took the chicken parts and put them into a big pot filled with water. She lit the oil burner and waited for the water to boil. Meanwhile, she prepared the vegetables by peeling the carrots and the parsnip roots and cutting them to three inches long. Next, she cleaned the onion and the celery roots. She took the dill and parsley leaves and tied them together with a thread so that later she would be able to pull them out from the soup. At this point, while the water warmed, Nacha lifted the cover and scooped the brown particles floating on the surface, which came from the chicken bones. Along with it, Nacha also scooped two cups of water that was replaced with boiled clear water. Once the water boiled, Nacha added the vegetables, salt, pepper, and two tablespoon of chicken powder. She let it continue to boil on low for an hour and a half. It was the best soup ever and it spread a delicious smell throughout the house!

GEFILTE FISH

The fish preparation was next in line. They bought it the previous day in the market with all other items. It was swimming happily in a big bucket with its friends when Nacha and Esther entered the store and chose their victim. The storekeeper had a long handle with a round net at the end to catch it. Once the fish was in his hand, he ended its life quickly with a strong hit on the head. Then, Esther sat on a low bench and peeled off its scales. The rest of the process was done delicately; only Mother had the skills and knowledge to cut it without touching the spleen. "Remember children," she used to say, "If you cut the spleen you will spoil the fish. It will be very bitter and inedible." With that statement, she sliced the fish.

Figure 21: Gefilte fish made by Yaffa's daughter-in-law, Melissa Liebermann, for a Rosh Hashanah dinner in 2020.

Part of the fish stayed sliced, and some went into the grinding machine. She added breadcrumbs, eggs, salt, pepper, and a little sugar to the ground fish and formed the mixture into balls. Some of the mix she cooked shaped as elliptical balls and some she stuffed the sliced fish with, then cooked it for half an hour. During the meal, it was presented as a piece of sliced fish filled with ground fish. That was where the name "gefilte fish," (stuffed fish) came from. On top of the fish ball, a colorful sliced cooked carrot was placed. Traditionally, the head of the family was served the fish's head and the rest ate the slices.

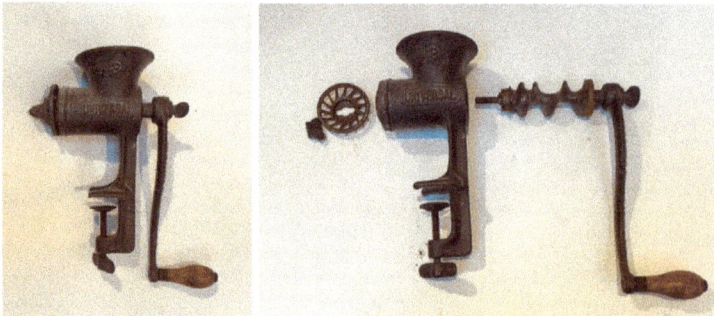

Figure 22: A meat and fish grinder assembled (left) and disassembled (right).

39

Making the Challah

Challah is a specific type of bread that symbolizes Shabbat. For Friday dinner, two challahs were placed at the head of the table on a special decorated plate covered with an embroidered cloth. It tastes different than regular bread because it is slightly sweeter and softer to welcome the Holy Shabbat with happiness and understanding.

The challah making was an adventure in and of itself. The first step was to prepare the yeast, a live organism that always fascinated Rachel because of the way it grew right in front of her eyes. When she made the challah, Mother used to say, "Do not forget to keep every utensil you use with the yeast at a warm temperature. The yeast needs warmth and a little sweetness; it will not grow in cold conditions."

Nacha put the flour and a teaspoon of salt in a big bowl. She made a well in the center and broke the egg into it. Then, she added the yeast mixture and stirred it with a wooden spoon, slowly pouring the warm water into the bowl to make a stiff dough. The dough was turned on the table, which was covered with flour, and kneaded until it was smooth and elastic.

Figure 23: Braided challah with sesame seeds.

The next step was to place it near the stove in a greased, warm bowl until it doubled in size. Two hours later, Nacha and Rachel separated the dough into six balls and rolled each one between their hands to make long strips. They braided three strips together and made two challahs and put them in a greased pan and left it to rise in the warm spot again.

The last step, before putting it in the oven, was to brush it with some beaten egg, so it became light brown and a little crusty. Sometimes sesame or poppy seeds was sprinkled on top. The baking was done two hours before the Shabbat dinner. The aroma of the baked challah spread throughout the entire house and welcomed the men when they returned on Friday night from the synagogue.

MAKING NOODLES

On the same surface that the challah was kneaded, the noodles for the soup were prepared. Without yeast, the dough was rolled onto the flat surface until it became as thin as possible. Then, Mother rolled it, sliced it with a sharp knife, and cooked it in lightly salted water. The noodles were thin and delicious, and everyone enjoyed their taste in the chicken soup.

THE "LEKACH" - POUND CAKE

Figure 24: Baking pan to put on a wick heating burner (Left). The opened baking pan (Middle). Sponge cake baked into the bunt pan and plated (right)

The "lekach" was a challenge to prepare. The first step was dividing the egg yolk from the egg whites. The second step was the most difficult: beating the egg whites. It was a labor of love and duty. Rachel sat on a low stool with the bowl in front of her. The secret was to steadily beat the eggs, adding small amounts of sugar at a time until it became a white, smooth, and stiff foam, so if she turned the bowl upside down, at the end, it would not fall out. In another bowl they mixed the rest of the ingredients. Once ready, they slowly poured the foam into a bowl and folded it with big motions as to not deflate the foam. The mixture was poured into a round baking pan and was placed on the stove to be baked slowly.

The children loved to peek through the little holes in the lid to see the cake rise. Mother used to stick a knife in the cake when she thought it was completely baked. It sat for twenty minutes and then was flipped onto a plate; a beautiful round-shaped cake appeared. It was a tasty addition to the afternoon tea that was served when the family woke up from their Shabbat afternoon nap.

"CHOLENT" SLOW COOKING - BEANS, POTATOES, AND MEAT

"Cholent" was the last item placed on the wood stove. It was a slow cooked stew that was put on the stove on Friday and was ready on Saturday. Every wife in the community cooked it the traditional way. However, it was adjusted to her own style and readjusted to satisfy the family's requests. The preparation for the cholent began on Thursday night when the beans were soaked in water. On Friday, Nacha counted the number of onions and potatoes, so each person got two potatoes. The girls helped with the peeling and cutting. The onions were diced and sautéed in oil, and the potatoes were cut into quarters proportional to the size.

Figure 25: Cooked cholent

Figure 26: Layering of the cholent starts with onion, then potatoes, and finally beans. Season with salt and pepper, then repeat the layers all over again until the pot is full.

42

Then, the layering of the cholent took place. Rachel loved to organize the ingredients in the pot. In the first layer were some sautéed onions, the second layer had the cut potatoes, and the third layer had the drained beans. In the middle, a good piece of meat with a bone was placed. Rachel repeated the same layering twice more, remembering that the secret for success was sprinkling salt and pepper on each layer.

"KISHKA": STUFFED CHICKEN NECK'S SKIN

Mother assembled the "kishka." She added flour to the leftover sautéed onions and mixed it with water, an egg, salt, and pepper. She stirred it well and stuffed it in the skin of a chicken's neck. She put it in the pot on the top of the cholent, covered it, put it on a hot flame for a few minutes until it boiled, and then moved it to the top of the stove to be cooked slowly throughout the night and day. The aroma of the cholent filled the house during the night and the morning. It was the smell that welcomed the men when they entered the home coming back from the synagogue.

Figure 27: Kishka dough is prepared by beating eggs, flour, onions, water, salt, and pepper. Then the dough is kneaded and stuffed into the skin of the chicken neck.

Figure 28: An unstuffed kishka can be cooked on top of the cholent in the stew pot.

Father and the boys had to make the "minyan" at the synagogue on time. A quorum of ten men over the age of thirteen were required to go to synagogue to complete traditional Jewish public worship. In the Lajzerowicz family, Joseph was the Cantor and conducted the ceremony alongside the Rabbi. Shimon-Binem, Joseph, Father Eliezer, and little Mordechai were in a hurry to put on their white shirts with their "kanfot tzitzit" (a piece of woven garment with an opening around the neck that has four fringes and a thread of blue, one in each corner) dangling outside the shirt. The fringes were a reminder to follow the Lord's paths, (from four corners of the world- North, South, West and East), and not to follow the heart or eyes that might lead one astray.

Figure 29: An iron powered by electricity and a scissor for tailoring.

Figure 30: A Singer sewing machine that was used at that time.

Everyone knew that they had to be in their nicest clothes with their best behavior, and they had to be punctual to the Friday service. This meant that clothes had to be mended and pressed. When the entire family tried to achieve this target at once, the house became a little crazy (but a good type of crazy). This kind of stress seemed to be happening before any "simcha" (celebration).

When the men and boys were ready, they went to synagogue with Rachel because she loved to listen to Joseph pray in front of the ark of the covenant. Mother, Nacha, Esther, and baby Shoshana stayed at home to prepare the table for Shabbat dinner, and they got to rest a bit before the men returned.

When sundown came, Nacha lit the two candles (she always had a head cover on) and recited the blessing while covering her eyes.

"Baruch Atah Adonai Eloheinu Melech Ha-Olam Asher Kidshanu Ba Mitzvotav Vzivanu Lhadlick Ner Shel Shabbat Kodesh." (Praised art thou, O Lord our God, King of Universe, who sanctified us through thy commandments and ordered us to light a candle for Shabbat.) Then she added quietly, "O God please give us another week without the Goyim (non-Jews) hitting us in the streets."

When finished, she said aloud, "A gitten (good) Shabbat," and gave each child a kiss for the holy day.

SETTING THE TABLE FOR FRIDAY NIGHT DINNER

Esther prepared the table by covering it with an embroidered tablecloth. The cloth was cross stitched with purple flowers and green leaves. The family knew they had to eat and drink without spilling a drop on the tablecloth. Every spot, even if washed carefully, would stain, and the family could not afford two of them.

For Friday night, the best meat dishes were put out, and the glasses sparkled in the light. The two challahs were placed near the head of the table on a special plate used for Shabbat. They were covered with a beautiful, embroidered cloth. A cutting knife, a small plate of salt, the kiddush cup, and a bottle of wine were all placed close to each other on the table.

When Esther heard voices coming from the street, she ran to her mother and said, "I can hear Joseph singing Lecha Dody Lickrat Kala (come my love, welcome the bride that it is the Shabbat)."

Figure 31: (left to right) Havdalah set, kiddush wine cup, and silver Shabbat candles.

Figure 32: Challah plate made by Yaffa 1986, two challahs, cover, wine, and kiddush cup.

Figure 33: Friday dinner blessing the Shabbat over the kiddush cup.

The men entered the home blessing the holy day with a happy "Shabbat Shalom" (have a peaceful Saturday). Father sat at the head of the table and Mother was on the opposite side. Shimon-Binem, the oldest son, sat on his right while Mordechai-Mayer sat on the left. The rest of the family sat wherever they wished. Father looked around at his children dressed up with clean and ironed shirts and the girls with beautiful dresses made for Yom Tov (The Sabbath and holidays). He felt so proud of his family, especially his wife, who stood, quietly waiting for the ceremony to start. He sang the traditional "Eshet Chail," praising his wife.

THE FRIDAY NIGHT MEAL

The family was sitting around the table when father gestured to stand up. He poured the wine into the kiddush cup and held it in front of him.

Before the traditional ceremony, he prayed, "Thank you, God, for giving us two weeks without any suffering from the locals. Please give us another peaceful week where we go about our own lives."

While standing and holding the kiddush cup in his hand, he recited the blessing to welcome the Sabbath.

"Thou didst choose us from among the peoples and in Thy love and favor didst sanctify us in giving us thy holy Shabbat as a joyous heritage. Baruch Atah Adonai Mekadesh Shabbat." (22)

The kiddush cup was passed to Nacha and then to each child, beginning with the eldest and ending with the youngest.

The next step was done in silence because no one was allowed to speak between drinking wine and blessing the challah. They washed their hands with a special cup with two handles. The purpose of two handles was to avoid the clean hand from touching the yet unwashed hand. The way they communicated was entertaining; eyes were darting, heads were nodding, hands were pointing, and sounds were made. All was done without a single spoken word and amazingly everyone followed the directions. They realized that words were not needed to simply communicate a message.

After they all gathered around the table again, Eliezer recited the blessing over the challah, "Baruch Atah Adonai Hamotzi Lechem Min Haaretz."

Then he cut part of the challah into small pieces, sprinkled it with salt, and put it in a special bowl. The pieces of the challah were passed around the table, then the rest of the meal was served. They had fish and clear chicken soup with homemade noodles. The chicken came with a side dish of cooked potatoes.

They ate compote, a very dense fruit soup, for dessert. Each meal ended with hot tea while sitting around the table using the best glasses with the silver handles, accompanied by a piece of pound cake.

Figure 34: Glasses for hot tea with silver holders.

Figure 35: A cup with two handles to wash hands.

Throughout the meal, between servings, the whole family sang the traditional "Zemirot Shabbat" (songs for Shabbat). Joseph was the leading figure as his voice was deep and full of passion; the family followed him with a beautiful melody. The meal ended with the blessing of the food: "Birkat Hamazon." With that, the family was ready to get a good night's sleep.

THE SHABBAT ROUTINE AND SYNAGOGUE SERVICE

On Shabbat morning, the Lajzerowicz family had a tradition of waking up, drinking hot tea, getting dressed, and walking across the square quickly to the synagogue. At that time, women came only for the last part of the service and sat in the balcony separated from the men (it was believed that the beauty of a woman could distract a man from focusing on the holy work of prayer). The result of this arrangement was good; everyone could concentrate and meditate at appropriate times, and the children could run up and down to check on each parent.

The boys are responsible for their own prayer once at age 13 once, they go through their Bar Mitzvah, the act of reading the Torah. Orthodox Jewish girls have their Bat Mitzvah celebration at age twelve, but they are required to recite our ancestors' wise words, not the Torah. They have it one year earlier because, according to tradition, girls mature earlier. Younger children have fun in the synagogue during prayers, they run in and out with other children, play hide and seek and enjoy the time. If some happy noise come from their side, no one cares. It is their time to act like children free of worries.

The Rabbi and Rachel's brother Joseph as the Cantor, led the service. When Joseph recited a part, his voice was so strong, powerful, and deliberate that it felt like he had truly opened the gate of Heaven and the rest of the voices followed.

Nacha recited three lines that she thought were the most important, "O Lord, guard my tongue from evil and my lips from speaking guile, and to those who slander me, let me give no heed. May my soul be humble and forgiving unto all."

After the service, people stayed for the "Kiddush" in the synagogue. A Kiddush is a spread of food that was served after the prayers in the adjusting room. This was an opportunity for the community to get together and celebrate milestones in each family's life. On that Shabbat, a Brith ceremony (a Jewish circumcision) for an eight-day-old baby took place; this occasion was a great celebration. For the

50

Kiddush, the family served what they could afford to purchase. On the table laid two big challahs, lekach (pound cake), schnapps (brandy), herring (marinated fish), and gefilte fish. People ate, drank, and talked.

After the Kiddush, everyone went home. When the Lajzerowicz men entered the house, the aroma of the cholent was the first thing they noticed. Father blessed the Sabbath over wine and challah. The cholent was served hot. It was brown from cooking overnight, and the potatoes and the beans were delicious. The best part of it all was the kishka, which was divided equally amongst everyone. Each person pretended that they were simply glancing casually at the kishka, but, truthfully, they were looking to ensure they got a fair share.

After the hungry family had the meal, Shimon-Binem gave an explanation on "Parashat-Hashavua," the Torah portion that was read in the synagogue that week. He talked about it like they were in biblical times but concluded his teaching by connecting the past and present. If mankind did not learn from the past, we would not learn how to live in the present or plan the future. Some family members asked questions, and some gave answers. It was a fulfilling conversation. Shabbat was a day of rest as well as a day of mental challenge. Father and Mother enjoyed the discussion around the table with a feeling of parental pride ran through their hearts, that was what they considered a real "Nachat" (translation from Yiddish for satisfaction or pride flowing through one's heart). The meal was concluded with hot tea and lemon to absorb the fat from the cholent, and "Birkat Hamazon," the blessing after the meal.

A good afternoon's sleep followed the meal, and when they woke up, the afternoon tea and "lekach" (pound cake) were served. Later in the day, Shimon-Binem directed the study of the Talmud in the synagogue. He was considered a great scholar, and people loved to listen to his lectures. The men stayed at the synagogue until "Mincha" and "Maariv" (the afternoon and evening services).

They arrived home at sundown. The "Havdalah" ceremony was held when three stars lit up in the sky. This is the time that the day ends, and night begins. Eliezer was holding the long-braided candle in one hand while he had the kiddush cup on a small silver plate in the other hand.

Mordechai-Mayer passed the spice box around so everyone would smell the sweet aroma.

Father recited the blessings, "Blessed art thou, O Lord our God, King of the Universe, who created the fruit of the vine. Blessed art thou, O Lord our God, King of the Universe, who created diverse kinds of spices. Blessed art thou, O Lord our God, King of the Universe, who created the light of the fire."

"Havdalah" means separation. The ceremony was guided to clearly separate this departing holy day from the coming ordinary weekday. It is a multi-sensory event of blessing over lights, wine or grape juice and smelling spice. It is an inspiring way to end Shabbath and start a new week.

"Praised be thou, O Lord, who marked a distinction between holy and profane."

They then inhaled the aroma that came from the spice box, and Father dipped the lit candle into the wine on the small plate. With that gesture, Shabbat was finished, and the regular work week began.

The Young "HeChalutz" - The Young Pioneer - Zionist Youth Movement in Zduńska Wola from 1932 to 1939

Figure 36: Zev (standing fifth from the right on the top row), Rachel's future husband, in the youth movement in Lithuania (1929).

A few youth movements were in Zduńska Wola. Yosef, one of Rachel's older brothers, and his girlfriend Pnina, joined the young HeChalutz because the movement's philosophy suited them. Its mission was to prepare pioneers seeking immigration to Palestine. It was conducted in three stages: 1) Join the local branch. 2) Prepare for a life in Israel in a community like a Kibbutz in Poland. 3) Move to Israel and help establish a Jewish state.

The local branches marketed their philosophy to the youngsters and wanted as many individuals as possible on their side. They had enthusiastic leaders from Israel who stayed for three to four years; after which, the leaders were exchanged with new ones. The weekly meetings in the branches educated the participants about Israel, and guest speakers visited to describe the current situation in Israel and its relationship to other countries. They had fun together through activities, singing, dancing, and dreaming about the future of the country. The philosophy was social Zionism: equal rights while learning to share and live in a commune. There were no higher or lower classes among the people in the group, and everyone learned Hebrew so they could function well in the new state. The final goal was moving to Israel, and it was named "Aliyah" (ascending) (23).

Figure 37: 1937 - Zev (sitting) building houses in Israel.

"Aliyah" means ascent. It is the immigration of Jews from the diaspora to the Land of Israel. It is also defined as "the act of going up" (towards Jerusalem). "Making Aliyah" by moving to Israel is one of the most fundamental components of Zionism. Someone who "makes Aliyah" is called an "oleh" (masculine) or "olla" (feminine). Many religious Jews think of "Aliyah" as a return to the Promised Land and believe it fulfills God's biblical promise to the descendants of the Hebrew patriarchs: Abraham, Isaac, and Jacob.

This passage in the Mishnah emphasizes the importance of living in Israel: "One should always live in the Land of Israel, even in a town most of whose inhabitants are idolaters, but let no one live outside the Land, even in a town most of whose inhabitants are Israelites; for whoever lives in the Land of Israel may be considered to have a God, but whoever lives outside the land may be regarded as one who has no God." (24)

The first step was being part of HeChalutz in the weekly meetings. The second step was to move to a Kibbutz in Poland, where members mimicked the work of a Kibbutz in Israel. They planted vegetables and fruit, raised cows, prepared milk and cheese, and - most importantly - learned how to live together. They had to stay in the Kibbutz for six months to a year, or, at least, through summer and winter to learn the effects of the changing seasons (25).

The third step was the Aliya (ascending) to Israel. Joseph and Pnina were eager to accomplish their dreams, and they were strongly supported by the family, who wished them well in their journey to a promising land. They went to Israel in 1934. They left behind their home, where they had no future, and went to an unknown country without family. They were young, courageous, full of dreams, and energetic to start a new life. In Israel, no one would prosecute them due to their religion, their accent, their look, or their clothes. They could finally be free to celebrate religious holidays in their own synagogue and to study and practice any profession or skill they wished to acquire.

Figure 39: Pnina, Joseph, and Rachel before they left for Israel (July 21, 1934).

Figure 40: 1936 – Rachel, fashionably dressed, with a friend

HISTORICAL POINTS WHY POLAND HATED THE JEWS

Economically, the great depression occurred around the world in 1929. The industry shrunk. People lost their jobs. Families had difficulty to feed themselves. Multiple times throughout history, whenever there was a shortage of food, an atmosphere of hatred developed against Jews. This time, the same disliking occurred again. At first, hate boiled under the surface, but it progressively became an organized incitement to eliminate as many Jews as possible.

It started when the government eliminated Jews' jobs and forced them into a lower status. Mobs would stand in front of Jewish stores stopping the Christian buyers from entering. The crowd boycotted Jewish merchandise until Jewish people became economically insecure, mentally challenged, and confused. They constantly wondered: why are Jews not treated as equals even though this is their home country?

The Polish government discussed the issue of having one million "unnecessary" Jews. The streets had posters saying, "Jews to Palestine or Madagascar" and announcing them as temporary residents. With growing anti-Semitism, the Jews had limited options. Some joined the extreme left, meaning the communist party. The Polish hand found most of them prosecuted, arrested, put them in jail, and killed them. The others died after they were sent to fight in the war with Spain.

Some Jews inclined toward the right and joined the revisionist movement. As a result of this change, the votes for the Jewish congress in 1933 resulted in 48,800 votes for the revisionist movement and 214,000 votes for organizations geared toward moving to Israel.

The Chalutz (a pioneer movement) was the biggest one of these organizations. This was the movement that Joseph, Pnina, and Rachel later joined as they followed their mission to immigrate to Israel. After the first World War, the Polish authority issued certificates for Jews to go to Israel, and 100,000 documented Jews immigrated between the two World Wars (26).

Joseph and Pnina moved to Israel; they made an Aliyah. In Israel, they worked in an orange grove, picking and sorting oranges. The better oranges they had wrapped in thin papers to be shipped abroad.

The regular ones they put for sale in the Israeli market. The couple toured the country by foot and on donkeys. They took photos and sent them to Rachel to convince her to join them. Joseph always insisted on writing the date and the location on the back of each picture, which is helpful when placing them in chronological order.

Figure 41: Pnina working in the orange grove (April 30th, 1937).

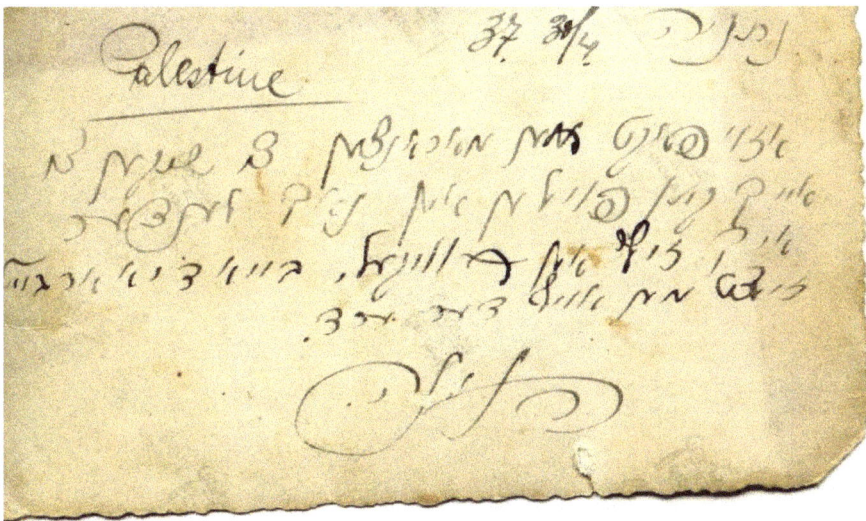

Figure 42: Inscription on the back of the picture in Figure 44.

Figure 43: Joseph and Pnina touring the dry land and meeting with an Arab friend (June 12, 1935).

WHY DID THEY MOVE TO ISRAEL?

Joseph and Pnina decided to move to Israel because of the discrimination against Jews at the time; there was no future for them in

Poland. The couple did not have any economical roots in the country, and small home businesses were diminishing. Usually, when parents built a business, their adult children took over with their new ideas and modernized the business to be more efficient. Since the family business became smaller, no additional workers were necessary.

Most of the Jews could not get a higher education. Universities had limited space for students. Parents were willing to pay the needed amount of money to send their children to university, but the doors were closed. If they managed to register, they were instructed to sit in the back of the room, and they faced harassment from other students. On top of these harsh conditions, when and if they completed their studies and got a degree, but most companies and firms refused to hire them.

Meanwhile, life in Israel was not easy. Joseph and Pnina had to learn new skills to receive an income. Some women made their own clothes and baked the bread for the week (challah for Friday), and people try to build their own houses. At the beginning, their home was a wooden shack. Eventually they built a house made of brick and cement.

When immigrant started to come to Israel, they saw a dry land with few residents living in the country. The wells in the desert were neglected by the locals for centuries, so they got clogged and became non-functional. The thirsty bushes dried, and the sand from the Negev's desert migrated north without vegetation to stop it. There was no running water, no irrigation, very little vegetation, and only a few trees and bushes. The "olim" (Jewish immigrants) were enthusiastic to rebuild the country. Nothing stopped them from proceeding forward step by step and solving any problems they encountered.

While Joseph and Pnina settled in Israel, Rachel continued to live in Zduńska Wola, studying at Bnot Yaakov high school and helping the family prepare milk, cheese, and wool. In the evenings, she joined the local branch of the HeChalutz. Rachel realized that she also had no future in Zduńska Wola. She needed to move to the big city of Lodz to study and gain skills to support herself. In parallel, she needed to search for a good husband and start a family.

WHY ANTI-SEMITISM IS ROOTED IN THE WORLD

THE JEWISH COMMUNITY

At the time, Jews had the nickname "wandering Jew" because they were always looking for a suitable place to raise a family. The Jews wanted to live peacefully, study, and practice their faith within the community. Most Jews worked hard, did not spend money on alcohol or unnecessary items, ate basic food, dressed respectable but simply, and saved money for education.

There were various types of Jews depending on their level of orthodox and place of residence. There were also many branches among the divisions which followed distinct leaders. Rachel was born into the orthodox group, but she became less strict as she grew older and left for Israel. The orthodox Jews lived in communities and married young, usually by a "shidduch" (matchmaker). According to religious rules, they were not allowed to experience any physical engagement with their partner prior to their marriage. They were not allowed to use contraceptives even after the marriage. They loved each child very much. The men devoted their time and energy to study the Torah and the Talmud, as a profession in the Yeshivah or after their work. The Jewish tradition is to continue these studies throughout life.

Orthodox Jewish education flourished in Poland. The Talmud was studied in Yeshivas, at home, during the week, and on holy days. Little children were asked to recite and explain what they had learned, while adults would challenge each other with questions to find correct interpretations of the Biblical sentences.

The Jews lived in communities, which kept their social life, stores, schools, and synagogues within close circles. They tried to coexist with Christians, but the phrase "love your neighbor as you love yourself" was not accepted by many Christians. Some days, the Poles let the Jews live their own lives, but other days, Jews were persecuted without reason. Jewish people never knew what to expect. What would be the excuse for the "pogrom" (attack and destruction)? Their present and future was always uncertain and hazy (27).

So, why does so much hate develop towards Jews? What is the root of anti-Semitism? Why has anti-Semitism escalated and not decreased over the centuries?

BLOOD LIBEL

Blood libel, also known as blood accusation, is the superstitious accusation that Jews sacrifice Christian children at Passover so they can use the child's blood for their matzah (unleavened bread). In Poland, at springtime, around the month of March, rivers and lakes thawed as the ice and snow melted. During that time, a body of a young child, who fell into the water and never was found, would surface. Immediately desperation would fall over the Jewish community. This happened before Passover, so it was convenient for the crowed to blame the Jewish people for drowning the baby. This accusation naturally was against Jews beliefs and practices. This hateful and erroneous claim often led to the persecution of Jews.

The blood libel accusation challenged the Jewish community in the Middle Ages when the Catholic church had most influence on people. It got buried when people progressed in their independence thinking. Then it revived again by the Nazis during the Second World War. Its origin was rooted in ancient concepts and therefore was irrelevant to the time period, yet the Nazis used this concept in anti-Jewish propaganda. They revived many unfair old claims about the Jews (28).

"LEGAL" JUSTICE

When a Jew was blamed for blood libel in Europe, there were certain "legal" steps that were followed to feign justice. 1) A Jew was "caught" and accused. 2) A Jew was tortured unbearably until he admitted to the accusation. 3) The pain was so forceful that the Jew was driven to "confess" that members of the community helped him. 4) The Jew was put on trial after "confessing". 5) With the forced confession, he was found guilty. 6) His belongings were taken to the accuser. Some people took advantage of this process. For example: It was beneficial to the bishop if the owner of the Jewish bank was accused. Then the church would be excused from returning the loaned money to the bank.

THE CATHOLIC CHURCH

The Catholic Church saw the Jews as a good target for income. Pious Catholics visited the church once or twice per day, accepted what their spiritual leader said, and followed it. If the Priest made negative claims against Jews, an outburst may follow in which Jews found themselves defenseless. Moreover, the church would often spend all the money it had because the priests lived off the income of the poor peasants. This was the point when the Priest would instigate people against Jews. After persecuting the Jews or forcing them out, the Priest would confiscate their money and use it to benefit himself and the church (29).

THE JEWISH MESSENGERS

In Poland, the Jews were the minions of Polish Kings and Dukes. Jews took taxes from the peasants and controlled the alcohol. These were reasons to hate the Jews, and this hate did not cease over history. Who likes the tax collector? Who likes to be prevented from drinking as much as they desire? Who likes to see their families hard-grown vegetables and fruits taken away to a rich person? The Polish village people did not hate their King or Duke because they did not see them. The royalty lived in a palace far from the community and their social lives did not connect to that of the villagers. Therefore, the Jewish money collectors were an easy target of blame. The Kings and Dukes benefited from the Jews as their dedicated worker because they helped them. The commoners despised Jews and attacked them, while the aristocracy was left untouched (30).

JEWS WERE DIFFERENT

The Jews were different, and people did not know how to accept differences. Orthodox Jewish children and adults dressed in long black coats and black hats of different shapes, materials, and styles. They always covered their heads: some of their hats were round with fur, some were cylinder-shaped, some were worn like a beret, and some were worn like a yarmulke. They also had "peots" -which were uncut sideburns that became a long and curly strand of hair that dangled in front of their ears. They wore white shirts and made sure that four "tzitzit" (four special knotted fringes that were attached in four corners to a "tallit katan," which was worn as undergarment) were always seen outside the shirt. Orthodox Jews also ate kosher food and usually did not invite non-Jews to their home. The women dressed in long dark dresses and married women wore head covers. They spoke mostly Yiddish (an old German dialect combined with Hebrew). Jews went to school starting at the age of three until they were eighteen (31).

NO PROPERTY FOR JEWS

The Jews were not allowed to own property. Therefore, because of this rule, Jews could not farm because if one grew trees or vegetables they were considered a landowner. As a result, Jews did not have any other option but to go into finance. Some families sold items on a cart walking in the streets, some owned stores and some established banks. Then they loaned to people to develop businesses. This alone generated jealousy within the town resulting in blind hate.

PREJUDICE PASSED DOWN FOR GENERATIONS

From the community around them, Christians learned from a young age that Jews were different from them. This knowledge was embedded in their minds as they grew up, evolving into a fixed prejudice that Jews were responsible for all hardship that the common people suffered. No one defended the Jews. Consequently, this kind of hate continued from generation to generation (32).

RACHEL'S MOVE TO LODZ IN 1938 TO EARLY 1939

Rachel's father, Eliezer, had a relative from Lodz who needed help in her bakery. She asked him if he knew someone that was willing to help her at the bakery. He suggested that Rachel could join her. He discussed this idea with Rachel and Mother, and they both agreed with Father: there was no job for Rachel in the milk and wool at hometown. The industry constantly developed technology to process the milk and weave the wool, so their income was diminishing rapidly. Nacha and Eliezer supported the idea of Rachel moving to Lodz, a big city in Poland with more opportunities to thrive. It helped that Rachel's older brother, Shimon-Binem, and his family resided in Lodz and would be there for her if she needed help. To celebrate her move to the promising city, Rachel's family and friends gathered together. All were sad to see her leave but wished her well and prayed that she would achieve her dreams. It was a big transition to leave her Zdunska Wola and go to a big city all alone, but Rachel did it courageously.

Figure 44: Rachel with her three sisters before leaving for Lodz (October 1st, 1938).

Figure 45: Rachel is moving to Lodz.

She rented a one-unit apartment near her brother. It had a bed, a bathroom, and a kitchen. Rachel immediately went to the bakery in the center of town. She loved her job and fit right in there. The owner of the bakery was appreciative of Rachel's ability to learn the trade of baking and to understand the importance of following the baking recipes step-by-step. Her co-workers respected her because Rachel never denied anyone's requests, and she was always searching for ways she could help. She was a team player and assisted others with baking, cleaning, and keeping the bakery appealing to the customers.

Figure 46: (left) Rachel, on the left, with a friend in Lodz (June 6, 1938); (right) Rachel with a group of friends in Lodz (July 1938). All dressed fashionably.

The move brought out one of Rachel's main characteristics: she was a down-to-earth person. She analyzed what would be the right thing to do and made the decision to follow through. She took steps into the unknown, which ultimately saved her life and rescued her from being burned in an Auschwitz crematorium. Her brother, Shimon-Binem faced this terrible fate, and his family that lived in Lodz was forced to move by the Nazis to the Lodz Ghetto and then to their final annihilation in Auschwitz.

THE BAKERY

When Rachel first entered the bakery, she realized that nothing smells as amazing as freshly baked dough. She observed a fascinating variety of countless breads displayed on the baker's rack. The most traditional bread was baked with wheat and rye flours, slightly sour from the leaven, or "zakwas" made without any yeast. There were others too. Some were white and fluffy (usually those were baked with more yeast) and others were heavy from all the bran. Some were savory and salty, while others went together with butter and jam. Some were sprinkled with poppy or sesame seeds, while others were spiced with caraway or nigella. There were also breads baked with buckwheat, millet, spelt, or oats. Some breads would surprise Rachel with fried onions while others had mixed raisins. There were also bread rolls. Some popular ones were "kajzerka" and the crispy "sznytka," healthy multigrain rolls filled with fried cheese and garlic butter to taste. The most popular ones were "paszteciki," which were either made with puff pastry or yeast dough and filled with sauerkraut and mushrooms, spinach, meat, or lentils. The selection was impressive. Rachel watched the operation and readied herself to learn the steps for successful baking following traditional Polish baking (33).

Figure 47: Rachel in Lodz (1938).

Figure 48: Rachel in the bakery.

She enjoyed going to the bakery every day, and she would work from dawn to dusk to help clean, prepare the dough for baking, and work at the counter selling bread. She stayed late until the shop closed and made sure it was clean for the next day. Customers liked to come to the bakery to buy bread and pastry but also to enjoy the smell, look at the beautiful pastries and taste of the bread. They enjoyed talking and spending time with the staff most of all.

Figure 49: Yaffa and Hadas visited Lodz in 2002 and enjoyed the beautiful old buildings and the people on the street.

EARLY 20TH CENTURY IN LODZ, POLAND

Jews were an integral part of the Lodz textile industry. They owned 175 factories by 1914. First World War had changed the industry and devastated the city of Lodz; many factories were destroyed, and Jewish industrialists were not given financial aid from the government to rebuild them. Anti-Jewish policies were enacted in the inter-war period. Nevertheless, Jews continued to work, and many were able to provide for their families.

The ready-made tailoring industry was almost entirely composed of Jewish tailors who were also active in other related businesses. The merchants formed a union while other smaller Jewish unions existed for the tradesmen and retailers. They all were an important part of the working forces to the extent that they were approached by the Bund, a Jewish socialist movement, as well as the Poalei Zion and Polish Socialist Party, for their votes for the Jewish Community Council of Lodz (34).

Jews also maintained a vibrant social life in Lodz. In 1924, the first democratic election for the Jewish community council of Lodz was established. The Jewish community was responsible for maintaining a kosher slaughterhouse, a mikveh, and education for poor and charitable organizations. In the inter-war period, a soup kitchen was open for the poor, as well as "bikur holim" (visiting the sick) societies. B'nai Brith had a lodge in Lodz in 1926 that supported ORT vocational schools, orphanages, and other cultural institutions. A diverse education network was established in Lodz during that period. Several yeshivas opened and taught in Polish and Hebrew languages.

The Reformed Movement had its own "chader" (a small class for elementary school children). The first Jewish gymnasium was built in Lodz in 1912. A Yiddesh language was established in 1918, and a Jewish school for girls was established in 1924. Several famous Jewish artists and writers were born or lived in Lodz. Arthur Rubinstein (1887-1983), a world-renowned pianist was born in Lodz, as well as the famous composer Aleksander Tansman and the poet Julian Tuwim. The city had its own Jewish drama and theater companies.

Zionism (The movement to ascend to Israel) spread to Lodz in the early 1900s, following the first Zionist Congress 1897. Zionists were involved in the revival of the Hebrew language and Jewish culture. Anti-Semitism became prevalent in the 1930s due to Nazi propaganda. Organized attacks wounded and killed Jews in April 1933, May 1934, and September 1935. Wealthy Jews were arrested in 1938, and guards were placed outside Jewish shops to prevent non-Jewish customers from entering (35).

Figure 50: Hadas, Rachel's granddaughter, by Ghetto Warsaw's wall (2002).

This is the city where Rachel thought she would find her future. She tried to join a university and get a higher education, but she was not accepted to any institute. She tried to find a soul mate but was unsuccessful. The census in Poland in 1931 revealed that 83% of Jewish women in Poland between the ages twenty to twenty-four were not married while only 63% of the rest of the non-Jewish women in Poland at that age group were single. Rachel was nineteen years old, and it was hard for her to find a husband.

The Jewish economic status in Poland explained why women in that age group had difficulty getting married. The men aspired to have a respectable income prior to asking for a woman's hand in marriage. Men wanted to have a skill that would enable them to provide for a family. However, Jews found it difficult to be accepted into universities or apprenticeships for non-Jews. Consequently, the boys could not obtain skills that enabled them to ask a woman to marry them. The other option for the men was to look for a woman with a "naidunia" (dowry), meaning a bride who came from a wealthy family that could help them start a business. Many women were not born into established families with a high income and they could not offer a dowry to the prospective husband (36).

From observing her surroundings and thinking about her future, Rachel understood what she had to do to fulfill her needs. She joined the HeChalutz branch in Lodz that had inspiring leaders who were excited to move to Israel. She developed good relationships with the branch members, men and women interested in immigrating to Israel. Her brother Joseph, who lived in Israel, continued to send her cards and letters begging her to join him in building the Jewish land. Over time, Rachel grew very fond of the idea of moving to Israel, and she made the final decision after she learned about the massacre on "Kristallnacht" ("Crystal Night").

Figure 51: The Nazis escorting the Jews in shame.

NAME		SEX	BIRTH DATE	OCCUPATION	GHETTO	ADDRESS		NOTES
LAJZEROWICZ	ABRAM	M	14/ 7/1908	ANGEST	KELM 11	4		MAGISTRA 12
LAJZEROWICZ	ABRAM ICEK	M	19/12/1903	ARBEITER	SULZF 25/27	6		SULZF 3	PRZ 2.1.42 DOM 34
LAJZEROWICZ	ABRAM IZAAK		/ /1927		SIEGFRIED 14	31		
LAJZEROWICZ	ABRAM JOSEK	M	31/8/1932	SCHUELER	REIGER 5/7	27		
LAJZEROWICZ	ABRAM LAJZER	M	17/1/1922	SCHNEIDER	FISCH 11	31		ALEXHOF 18
LAJZEROWICZ	ABRAM MENDEL	M	15/ 1/1904		SULZF 18	2		
LAJZEROWICZ	ABRAM RAFAEL	M	28/1/1903	ARBEITER	SULZF 77	7		SULZF 75	WYM 21.6.42 BLEI 9
LAJZEROWICZ	ABRAM RAFAL	M	28/1/1903	ARBEITER	BLEI 9	15		SULZF 77
LAJZEROWICZ	ABRAM WOLF	M	/ /1888		ALEXHOF 24	27		
LAJZEROWICZ	ADELA	F	/ /1905	SCHNEIDERIN	HANSEAT 48	23		PABIANICE	AG 7.7.44
LAJZEROWICZ	ALEKSANDER	M	12/9/1883	INGENIEUR	HOHENS 40	8		JULIUS 13
LAJZEROWICZ	ALTA HENA	F	8/12/1912	HAUSFRAU	KORN 13	1		PABJANICK 6
LAJZEROWICZ	ARON	M	/ /1869		ALEXHOF 6	68		
LAJZEROWICZ	ARON ICEK	M	3/1/1923		ALEXHOF 33	36		
LAJZEROWICZ	BAJLA HINDA	F	6/ 7/1910	SCHNEIDERIN	MATROSEN 77	13		RUNDE 11	GEST 2.6.43
LAJZEROWICZ	BASIA	F	19/02/1925	ARBEITERIN	BRAUNE 14	5		KOLONIA MARYSIN
LAJZEROWICZ	BELA	F	14/ 5/1916	HAUSFRAU	KRIMHILD 22	2		A HITLER 41 WYM 1.9.40 KONIGSB
LAJZEROWICZ	BELA	F	14/ 5/1916	SCHNEIDERIN	KONIGSB 4	8		A.G. 30.6.44
LAJZEROWICZ	BINEM	M	12/1/1928	SCHUELER	RAUCH 27	15		LOWENSTADT AUSG 12.9.42
LAJZEROWICZ	BLUMA	F	8/12/1918	SCHNEIDERIN	RUNDE 11	17		ALEXHOF 11
LAJZEROWICZ	BLUMA	F	/ /1929	KIND	PFEFFER 15	106		A.M.	GEST 16.7.43
LAJZEROWICZ	BORUCH	M	7/ 4/1916	FRISEUR	HOLZ 36	26		PILSUD 14	WYM. 27.11.41 A.G.
LAJZEROWICZ	BRANDLA	F	/ /1884		SULZF 15	4		
LAJZEROWICZ	CHAIM	M	15/11/1906	KRAWIEC	FRANZ 12	14A		WYM 16.11.42 PIEPRZA
LAJZEROWICZ	CHAIM DAWID	M	/ /1930	SCHUELER	HAMBURG 14	32		MARYSIN KOL
LAJZEROWICZ	CHAIM ELIEZER		/ /1926		SIEGFRIED 14	31		
LAJZEROWICZ LAJFER	CHAJA	F	14/4/1908		FRANZ 38	40		
LAJZEROWICZ	CHAJA	F	/ /1923	HAUSFRAU	ALEXHOF 50	9		UJAZD
LAJZEROWICZ	CHAJA	F	28/ /1928	SCHUELERIN	BAL RING 3	2		BEST ? 21
LAJZEROWICZ	CHAJA	F	7/12/1922		ALEXHOF 50	9		
LAJZEROWICZ	CHAJA	F	/ /1901		ALEXHOF 33	36		
LAJZEROWICZ	CHAJA DWOJRA	F	/ /1914	GORSESTSCHNEID	HOLZ 36	26		PILSUD 14	WYM. 15.11.41 A.G.
LAJZEROWICZ	CHAJA FRYMET	F	27/ 7/1926	SCHNEIDERIN	KIRCHPL 4	27		BURSA MARYSIN
LAJZEROWICZ	CHAJA MALKA	F	/ /1924	HAUSTOCHTER	STEINMETZ 2	2		OST 17	AUSG 28.3.42
LAJZEROWICZ	CHAJA SURA	F	/ /1889		ALEXHOF 24	27		
LAJZEROWICZ	CHANA	F	/ /1908	HAUSFRAU	MUEHL 22	25		GLOCZNA 58 AG 30.6.44
LAJZEROWICZ	CHANA	F	/ /1931	KIND	PFEFFER 14	15		HANSEATEN 4
LAJZEROWICZ	CHANA	F	10/4/1911	HAUSFRAU	SULZF 11	15A		A.M.
LAJZEROWICZ	CHANA	F	/ /1924		ALEXHOF 35	28		
LAJZEROWICZ	CHANA LEJA	F	5/2/1907	HAUSFRAU	SCHLOSS 12	10		UJAZD	AUSG TR 10
LAJZEROWICZ	CHELA	F	3/7/1942	KIND	HOHENS 14	30		NEUGEB	AUSG 10.9.42
LAJZEROWICZ	CHIEL	M	18/7/1941		HAMBURGER 42	18		AUSG 4.9.42
LAJZEROWICZ	CHIL	M	3/1/1907	ZAHNTECHNIK	SATTLER 5	33		MUEHL 77	3.11.42
LAJZEROWICZ	CHIL	M	3/2/1907	ZAHNTECHNIK	MUHL 77	15		DANZIGER 24 WYM 1.11.42 SATTLER
LAJZEROWICZ	CHIL MAJER	M	15/8/1891	BIEGLER	FISCH 15	6		SUD 24	ABG 15.12.42 HAMB 4?
LAJZEROWICZ	CHIL MAJER	M	15/8/1897	SCHNEIDER	HAMBURGER 42	25		FISCH 15	GEST 23.3.43
LAJZEROWICZ	CYREL	F	16/1/1908	SCHNEID	AM BACH 29	47		ZACHODNA 18 27.7.44 HOHEN 10
LAJZEROWICZ	CYRLA	F	/ /1905	HAUSFRAU	HAMBURGER 63	5		HAMBURGER 63 8.1.43
LAJZEROWICZ	CYRLA	F	/ /1926	SCHUELERIN	SULZF 16	10		KONSKA	AUSG 20.3.42 TR 11/?
LAJZEROWICZ	CYRLA	F	/ /1908		AM BACH 29	47		
LAJZEROWICZ	CYWJA	F	14/4/1932	SCHUELERIN	FISCH 13	1		SCHLAGETER 58
LAJZEROWICZ	DAWID	M	16/8/1877	MAENDLER	FRANZ 34	15		BERLINER 15 AUSG 1.3.42 TR 14/?
LAJZEROWICZ	DAWID	M	17/11/1908	SCHUHMACHER	INSEL 19	4		FISCH 1
LAJZEROWICZ	DAWID	M	/ /1884		SULZF 16	10		
LAJZEROWICZ	DAWID LAJB	M	30/8/1873		ALEXHOF 35	28		ALEXHOF 44 A.G. TR VI
LAJZEROWICZ	DAWID MOSZEK	M	18/9/1939		ALEXHOF 26	53		A.G. 10.9.42
LAJZEROWICZ	DAWID SZYMON	M	10/7/1884	STRUMPFARBEITER	SULZF 16	10		HOHENS 80	GEST 23.3.42
LAJZEROWICZ	DINA	F	28/9/1916	WAESCHNAEH	FRANZ 6	15		PABJANICE	WYM 18.3.43 DABROWA
LAJZEROWICZ	DINA	F	10/5/1921	SCHNEIDERIN	SCHNEIDER 5	13		DABROWA	4.9.43
LAJZEROWICZ MEDALJA DORA		F	/ /1905	SCHAFTELMACHER	HAMBURG 15	10		FRANZ 20	AG 30.6.44
LAJZEROWICZ	DWOJRA LIBA	F	1/3/1891		ALEXHOF 35	28		
LAJZEROWICZ	ELEAZAR	M	20/12/1932		INSEL 19	4		FISCH 1
LAJZEROWICZ	ELKA	F	10/1/1920		ALEXHOF 33	36		
LAJZEROWICZ	ESTER MINDLA	F	15/1/1935	KIND	SCHLOSS 12	10		UJAZD	AUSG TR 10
LAJZEROWICZ	ESTERA	F	18/9/1909	HANDELSGEHILF	SULZF 18	2		SULZF 20
LAJZEROWICZ POZNANS ESTERA		F	12/1/1891		SULZF 40	61		KRAUTER 13
LAJZEROWICZ	ESTERA	F	/ /1910	STRICKERIN	HANSEATEN 27	61		SUDETEN 20 WYM 18.5.42 TOWIAN
LAJZEROWICZ	ESTERA	F	9/ 7/1910	STICKERIN	KELM 40	29		BLECH 4	ZAM 7.1.42
LAJZEROWICZ	ESTERA	F	18/9/1909	HANDELSGEHILFE	SULZF 18	18		SULZF 20	AUSG 19.1.42
LAJZEROWICZ	ESTERA	F	/ /1874	HAUSWIRTIN	SULZF 3			GEST 11.1.42
LAJZEROWICZ	ESTERA	F	24/6/1900	SCHNEID	AM BACH 29	47		ZACHODNA 18 14.7.44 HOHEN 10/5
LAJZEROWICZ	ESTERA	F	/ /1909		AM BACH 29	47		
LAJZEROWICZ POZNAWCKA ESTERA		F	15/3/1877		SULZF 40	61		KRAUTER 13 5.8.42
LAJZEROWICZ	ESTERA CHAJA	F	/ /1933	SCHUELERIN	HAMBURG 14	32		MARYSIN KOL
LAJZEROWICZ	ESTERA MALA	F	8/11/1898	HAUSFRAU	MUHL 63	1		STEIN 8	ABG 3.3.43 MUHL 59
LAJZEROWICZ	ESTERA RYWKA	F	1/4/1928		ALEXHOF 33	36		
LAJZEROWICZ	EZRYEL	M	1/1/1914	GLASER	HAMBURGER 9	18		MARTYNARSKA 21A AUSG 15.6.42 TR
LAJZEROWICZ PILATER IYSKA		F	19/9/1942	KIND	FISCH 15	1		NEUG	GEST 22.9.42
LAJZEROWICZ AJJENBAUM ESTERA MALA		F	/ /1899	HAUSFRAU	MUHL 59	11		MUHL 63	5.3.43
LAJZEROWICZ IZRAELO DOBA		F	14/ 5/1897	HAUSFRAU	HOLZ 35	10		A.M.	GEST. 9.6.42
LAJZEROWICZ KLEGOLD REGINA		F	29/ 1/1882	LEHRERIN	INSEL 32	51		KURZE 17
LAJZEROWICZ MENCING MALKE LAJE		F	19/5/1918	HAUSFRAU	HOHENS 14			LINDEN 3	PRZ 4.7.43
LAJZEROWICZ PROSZARSKA RYWKA JACHWETA		F	/ /1892	NAEHERIN	ALEXHOF 26	13		ALEXHOF 26
LAJZEROWICZ RADOMSK IDES		F	10/ 3/1907	HAUSFRAU	KELM 81	6		GOLDSCHM 23 ZAM 8.1.42
LAJZEROWICZ RAJMERM GUCIA		F	/ /1899	HAUSFRAU	KELM 77	9		RUNGE 4
LAJZEROWICZ SPIEWAK HINDA BAJLA		F	/ /1864	HAUSFRAU	REMBRANDT 4	18		BRZEZINSKA WYM 30.12.41 REM
LAJZEROWICZ	FAJGA	F	12/10/1919	SCHNEIDERIN	SIEGFR 33	11		HOLZ 36	ABG BLEI 24
LAJZEROWICZ	FAJGA	F	12/10/1919	SCHNEIDER	BLEI 24	4		SIEGFRIED 33
LAJZEROWICZ	FAJWEL MAJER	M	/ /1921		RUBENS 4	54		A.M.	GEST 24.7.42
LAJZEROWICZ	FRAJDLA	F	2/ 8/1886	SCHNEIDERIN	HOLZ 36	26		PILSUD 14

- 1432 -

Figure 52: 1942 - The Lajzerowicz family's second document from the ghetto in Lodz.

75

NAME		SEX	BIRTH DATE	OCCUPATION	GHETTO ADDRESS		NOTES
LAJZEROWICZ	FRAJDLA LAJA	F	23/ 7/1906	SPULERIN	KELM 9	2	KRIMHILD 9 WYW 12.2.42 FRANZ 40
LAJZEROWICZ	FRYMET	F	20/10/1909	HAUSFRAU	HAMBURGER 42 18		HAMBURGER 42 AUSG 11.9.42
LAJZEROWICZ	FRYMETA	F	13/ 3/1910	BUROANGEST	KELM 11	4	MAGISTR 12
LAJZEROWICZ	GITLA	F	/ 1902	HAUSFRAU	FISCH 13	1	SCHLAGETER 58
LAJZEROWICZ	GITLA	F	30/7/1896		HANSEATEN 61 41		PRZEJARD 47 AUSG 1.3.42 TR 8/2
LAJZEROWICZ	GITLA	F	15/1/1902	HAUSFRAU	SULZF 77	7	SULZF 75 WYM 21.6.42 BLEI 9
LAJZEROWICZ	GOLDA	F	/ 1905	HAUSFRAU	STEINMETZ 2 2		OST 17 AUSG 28.3.42
LAJZEROWICZ	GOLDA	F	/ 1892	HAUSFRAU	PFEFFER 7	8	ZACHODNIA 3 3.6.42 WARSCHAU
LAJZEROWICZ	GUCIA	F	/ 1903	HAUSFRAU	KELM 77	9	RUNGE 4 27.10.42
LAJZEROWICZ	GUTA	F	28/5/1908		ALEXHOF 24	27	
LAJZEROWICZ	HALINA	F	11/7/1932		HOHENS 40	8	JULIUS 13
LAJZEROWICZ	HALINA	F	9/4/1926	SCHUELERIN	MUHL 7	12	CEGILNIANA 23 ABG 30.12.42 HOLZ 8
LAJZEROWICZ	HANA	F	/ 1931		HANSEATEN 4 53		PFEFFER 21 ABG 15.7.42 PFEFFER 1
LAJZEROWICZ	HANA RUCHLA	F	5/12/1905	HAUSFRAU	REITER 11	25	ALEXHOF 47 20.10.43
LAJZEROWICZ KIBEL	HANA RUCHLA	F	5/12/1905	25HAUSFRAU	REITER 11		ALEXHOF 47 20.10.43
LAJZEROWICZ	HENIA	F	27/ 9/1927	SCHUELERIN	KIRCHG 3	28	MATROSEN 1 ZAM 19.1.42
LAJZEROWICZ	HERSZ	M	19/1/1895		ALEXHOF 33	36	
LAJZEROWICZ	HERSZ LAJB	M	15/12/1919	SCHNEIDER	SULZF 40	61	HOHENS 72 12.7.42
LAJZEROWICZ	HINDA RAJLA	F	/ 1864	HAUSFRAU	REMBRANDT 12 24		REMBRANDT 4 AUSG 5.3.42
LAJZEROWICZ	HIRSZ LAJB	M	15/12/1919	HANDELSGEHILFE	HOHENS 72	25	KRAUTER 13/47 AUSG TR 25
LAJZEROWICZ	ICEK	M	/ 1924	SCHUELER	STEINMETZ 2 2		OST 17 AUSG 28.3.42
LAJZEROWICZ	ICEK AKIWA	M	/ 1902	HAUSWAECHTER	HANSEATEN 4 53		PFEFFER 21 ABG 15.7.42 PFEFFER 1
LAJZEROWICZ	IDEL	M	7/11/1898	INTROLIGATOR	MUHL 63	1	STEIN 8 ZMARL 9.6.41
LAJZEROWICZ	IDES	F	10/11/1922	ARBEITERIN	HAMBURG 14	32	SUD 46
LAJZEROWICZ	IDESA	F	/ 1894		SULZF 20	7	SULZF 3 GEST 1.4.44
LAJZEROWICZ	ISRAEL	M	15/7/1897	BUROANGEST	MUHL 7	12	CEGILNIANA 23 ABG 30.12.42 HOLZ 8
LAJZEROWICZ	ITA LIBA	F	3/11/1916	ARBEITERIN	HAMBURGER 14 32		SUD 46
LAJZEROWICZ	IZRAEL	M	15/7/1897		HALBE 8	24	MUHL 7 31.12.42
LAJZEROWICZ	IZRAEL	M	25/8/1922	WIRKER	HOHENS 46	34	HOHENS 78
LAJZEROWICZ	IZRAEL	M	13/1/1899		MUHL 47	19	RZGOWSKA 18
LAJZEROWICZ	IZRAEL	M	/ 1925	SCHUELER	SULZF 16	10	HOHENS 80 AUSG 20.3.42 TR 11/2
LAJZEROWICZ	IZRAEL	M	25/8/1922	WORKER	HOHENS 46	34	HOHENS 78/17 4.11.42
LAJZEROWICZ	IZRAEL LAJB	M	/ 1936	KIND	SCHMIEDE 3	5	MUEHL 54 ANG. 5.12.43
LAJZEROWICZ	IZRAEL SENDER	M	19/4/1920	ARBEITER	HAMBURGER 42 3		SUD 13 ABG 8.2.43 CRANACH 34
LAJZEROWICZ	J MORDKA	M	/ 1925		SULZF 16	10	
LAJZEROWICZ	JAKOB NUSEN	M	10/10/1914	BUROANGEST	SULZF 40	61	KRAUTER 13 12.7.42
LAJZEROWICZ	JAKOB SZLAMA	M	1/ 1/1919	KIND	KORN 13	1	PABJANICK 6 AUSG 7.9.42
LAJZEROWICZ	JANKIEL	M	/ 1933		HANSEATEN 4 53		PFEFFER 21 ABG 15.7.42 PFEFFER 1
LAJZEROWICZ	JANKIEL	M	/ 1939	KIND	PFEFFER 14	15	HANSEATEN 4
LAJZEROWICZ	JANKIL DAWID	M	/ 1884		SIEGFRIED 14 31		
LAJZEROWICZ	JENTA	F	28/10/1905		FRANZ 38	83	SULZF 7
LAJZEROWICZ	JOJNE	M	15/3/1911	SCHNEIDER	FRANZ 61	48	AM BACH 25 GEST 8.3.42
LAJZEROWICZ	JOJNE	M	1/2/1911	SCHNEIDER	AM BACH 25	15	RZGOWSKA 105 FRANZ 64
LAJZEROWICZ	JOSEF	M	3/2/1884	KAUFMAN	HAMBURGER 14 32		SUD 46 GEST 3.1.43
LAJZEROWICZ	JOSEF	M	/ 1885		SULZF 15	4	
LAJZEROWICZ	JOSEF BER	M	22/12/1938		MUHL 77	15	DANZIGER 24 AUSG 10.9.42
LAJZEROWICZ	JOSEF HERSZ	M	/ 1924	SCHUELER	PFEFFER 15	106	ABG PFEFFER 17
LAJZEROWICZ	JOSEF SRULEM	M	8/12/1875	WEBER	KORN 13	1	PABJANICK 6 GEST 29.6.42
LAJZEROWICZ	JOSEF SZYMON	M	/ 1929		SIEGFRIED 14 31		
LAJZEROWICZ	JOSEK	M	1/6/1919		ALEXHOF 24	27	
LAJZEROWICZ	JOZEF	M	28/ 6/1937		KELM 77	9	RUNGE 4 GEST 2.2.43
LAJZEROWICZ	JUDA	M	22/10/1894	SCHNEIDER	RAUCH 27	15	LOWENSTADT GEST 17.8.42
LAJZEROWICZ	JUDIA	F	17/7/1939		FISCH 11	18	MOLTKE 39
LAJZEROWICZ	JUDKA MORDKA	M	2/12/1906	ELEKTROTECHNIK	ALEXHOF 6	68	ALEXHOF 39
LAJZEROWICZ	KIWE	M	/ 1910		AM BACH 27	22	
LAJZEROWICZ	LAJA	F	21/4/1937	KIND	FRANZ 38	83	AUSG 8.9.42
LAJZEROWICZ	LAJA	F	15/7/1923	WAESCHNAEHERIN	MUHL 18	24	MATROSEN 42 19.9.42
LAJZEROWICZ	LAJA	F	2/ 3/1940	KIND	KELM 81	6	GOLDSCHM 23 AUSG 12.9.42
LAJZEROWICZ	LAJA	F	/ 1905	VERKAUFERIN	KIRCHPL 1/3	3	HOHENS 5
LAJZEROWICZ	LAJA	F	11/ 3/1925		SULZF 7	35	
LAJZEROWICZ	LAJB	M	20/12/1907	ARBEITER	KIRCHG 3	28	MATROSEN 1 ZAM 19.1.42
LAJZEROWICZ	LAJB	M	/ 1910		SIEGFRIED 14 32		
LAJZEROWICZ	LAJB HERSZ	M	14/6/1900	BUEROANGEST	BAL RING 3	2	GAERTNER 1
LAJZEROWICZ	LAJBUS	M	3/3/1931	SCHUELER	ALEXHOF 33	36	
LAJZEROWICZ	LAJZER	M	30/3/1912	FRISEUR	FRANZ 61	48	HEER 98 AUSG 12.4.42
LAJZEROWICZ	LEBUSZ JOSEK	M	30/10/1881	SCHUHMACH	FRANZ 61	48	HEER 98 2MARL 5.10.41
LAJZEROWICZ	LEJB ABE	M	23/1/1934	KIND	SIEGFR 6	13	AM AUSG 28.3.42 TR 39
LAJZEROWICZ	LEJBUSZ	M	3/3/1931		ALEXHOF 33	36	
LAJZEROWICZ	LENA	F	18/ 2/1933		KONIGSB 4	8	A.G. 26.6.44
LAJZEROWICZ	LIBA	F	17/2/1916	SCHNEIDERIN	SIEGFR 33	11	HOLZ 36 ABG BLEI 24
LAJZEROWICZ	LIBA	F	17/7/1907	HAUSFRAU	SIEGFR 6	13	LIND 68 AUSG 28.3.42 TR 39
LAJZEROWICZ	LIBA	F	/ 1889		ALEXHOF 24	27	
LAJZEROWICZ	LOBA	F	/ 1930	SCHUELERIN	STEINMETZ 2 2		OST 17 AUSG 28.3.42
LAJZEROWICZ ZLOTNIK SZMUL		M	18/12/1885	WEBER	KRAUTER 22	6-7	KRAUTER 22 AUSG TR 9
LAJZEROWICZ	MAJER	M	28/5/1910	BAECKER	FRANZ 38	112	REPPEN 11.2.43
LAJZEROWICZ	MAJER LAJZER	M	1/4/1923		ALEXHOF 35	28	A.G. TR VI
LAJZEROWICZ	MALKA	F	/ 1920	STRUMPFARB	HAMBURGER 42 3		SUD 13 AUSG APRIL 42
LAJZEROWICZ	MALKA	F	28/6/1919	WAESCHENAEHERI	BAL RING 10	8	KOENIGSB 20 A.G.
LAJZEROWICZ	MALKA	F	28/ 6/1919	HAUSFRAU	KONIGSB 20	1	KORN 14 WYM 9.7.41 BAL-RING 1
LAJZEROWICZ	MALKA	F	28/6/1909		ALTMARKT 15	17	
LAJZEROWICZ	MANIA	F	/ 1918		STEINMETZ 9 40		STASZICA 6 AUSG 21.3.42 TR 19
LAJZEROWICZ	MAREJM SURA	F	/ 1913	BUROANGEST	HAMBURG 42	3	LITZMAN 7 ABG 18.7.44 HAMBURG 1
LAJZEROWICZ	MARIA	F	/ 1913	SCHUELERIN	SULZF 25/27	6	SULZF 3 25.6.42
LAJZEROWICZ	MARIEM SURA	F	11/4/1913		HAMBURG 12	3	HAMBURG 23 21.7.44
LAJZEROWICZ	MARJA	F	16/ 1/1912	BUCHALTER	INSEL 32	51	KURZE 17
LAJZEROWICZ	MARJEM SURA	F	/ 1913	ARBEITERIN	HAMBURGER 42 3		LITZMAN 7
LAJZEROWICZ	MASZA	F	20/12/1912	HAUSFRAU	MUHL 77	15	DANZIGER 24 AUSG 10.9.42
LAJZEROWICZ	MASZA	F	/ 1913	SCHNEIDERIN	KRAUTER 1/3	7	PABIANICE 27.5.42
LAJZEROWICZ	MENDEL	M	23/12/1910	SCHUMACHER	MUHL 3	11	LUTNIOW 7 UMG 4.10.42
LAJZEROWICZ	MENDEL	M	6/9/10		HOHENS 24	53	WIELUX 2 ABG 27.11.42 MUHL 3

- 1433 -

Figure 53: 1942 - The Lajzerowicz family's third document from the ghetto in Lodz.

KRISTALLNACHT" ("CRYSTAL NIGHT")

On November 9th and 10th in 1938, in riots known as "Kristallnacht," Nazi mobs torched and vandalized hundreds of synagogues throughout Germany. They damaged and destroyed thousands of Jewish homes, schools, businesses, hospitals, and cemeteries. Nearly a hundred Jews were murdered during the violence. Nazi officials ordered German police officers and firemen to do nothing as the riots raged and buildings burned. The firefighters were allowed to extinguish blazes that threatened Aryan-owned property.

In the immediate aftermath of Kristallnacht, the streets of Jewish communities were littered with broken glass from vandalized buildings, giving rise to the name "The Night of Broken Glass." The Nazis held the German-Jewish community responsible for the damage and imposed a collective fine of $400 million (in 1938 rates), according to the U.S.A. Holocaust Memorial Museum. Additionally, more than 30,000 Jewish men were arrested and sent to the Dachau, Buchenwald, and Sachsenhausen concentration camps in Germany. Concentration camps were specifically constructed to hold Jews, political prisoners, and other perceived enemies of the Nazi state.

German-Jews were subjected to repressive policies since 1933, when Nazi Party leader Adolf Hitler (1889-1945) became chancellor of Germany. However, prior to Kristallnacht, these Nazi policies were primarily nonviolent. After Kristallnacht, conditions for German-Jews grew increasingly worse. During World War II (1939-1945), Hitler and the Nazis implemented their so-called "Final Solution" to what they referred to as the "Jewish problem." They carried out systematic murder of Jewish people in gas chambers and crematoriums.

Six million European Jews died in what came to be known as the Holocaust. As mentioned before, this was the situation in Europe that led Rachel to leave Poland and immigrate to Israel, the Promise Land for Jews (37).

Figure 54: The synagogue being attacked and burned.

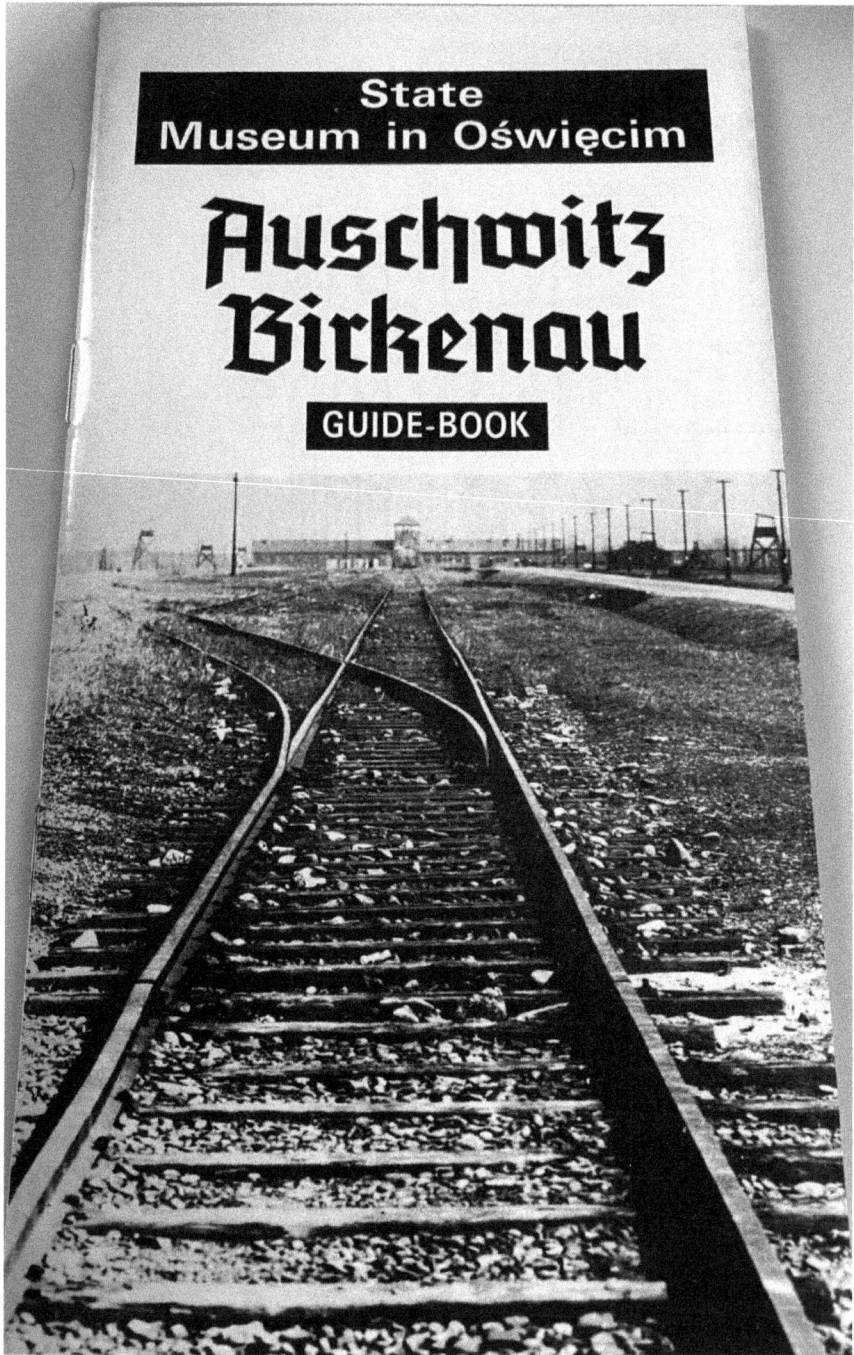

Figure 55: Yaffa and Hadas visited both Auschwitz and Birkenau Nazi's concentration camps where some of the 6,000,000 Jews were killed during World War II.

Figure 56: Yaffa and Hadas visited both Auschwitz and Birkenau Nazi's concentration camps where many of the 6,000,000 Jews were killed during World War II.

ISRAEL THROUGH THE YEARS (1915-1938)

The Jewish people were scattered all over the world since the destruction of the second temple in Israel in 70 CE. They were exiled from their home land to the diaspora and since then they did not have a state or country of their own. For thousands of years in their prayers, they wanted to come back to their promised land. Palestine was under British Mandate from 1917-1948 when the state became independent under the name Israel. The Zionist organizations were established with the goal of building a Jewish home land in Palestine since the late 19th century.

In 1917, British Foreign Secretary Arthur Balfour stated in a letter to British Jewish community leader Walter Lord Rothschild that:

"His Majesty's government view with favour the establishment in Palestine of a national home for the Jewish people, and will use their best endeavours to facilitate the achievement of this object, it being clearly understood that nothing shall be done which may prejudice the civil and religious rights of existing non-Jewish communities in Palestine, or the rights and political status enjoyed by Jews in any other country."

Through this letter, which became known as the Balfour Declaration, British government policy officially endorsed Zionism (38).

During World War I, the Jewish population declined in Palestine because of the war, famine, disease, and expulsion. In 1915, approximately 83,000 Jews lived in Palestine among 590,000 Muslim and Christian Arabs. According to the 1922 census, the Jewish population was 84,000, while the Arabs numbered 643,000. Thus, the Arab population continued to grow exponentially while that of the Jews stagnated.

In the mid-1920s, Jewish immigration to Palestine increased primarily because of anti-Jewish economic legislation in Poland and Washington's imposition of restrictive quotas. The record number of immigrants in 1935 was a response to the growing persecution of Jews in Nazi Germany. The British administration considered this number too large, so the Jewish Agency was informed that less than one-third of the quota it asked for would be approved in 1936 (39).

The British limited the absorptive capacity of Palestine by partitioning the country. In 1921, Colonial Secretary Winston Churchill awarded Sheriff Hussein's son Abdullah for his contribution to the war against Turkey. As a consolation prize for the Hejaz and Arabia going to the Saud family, Churchill installed him as emir. It severed nearly four-fifths of Palestine—some 35,000 square miles—to create a brand-new Arab emirate, Transjordan. The British went further and placed restrictions on Jewish land purchases in what remained of Palestine, contradicting the provision of the Mandate Article that stated:

"The Administration of Palestine...shall encourage, in cooperation with the Jewish Agency...close settlement by Jews on the land, including State lands and waste lands not acquired for public purposes." (40)

This made for Jewish acquisition of immigration certificates extremely difficult. As the world entered the Second World War, requests for entry were difficult to accommodate for Jews all over the world. Correspondence between governing officials in Palestine and Greek Jewish authority demonstrate the sheer inflexibility. Ultimately, the British admitted the argument about the absorptive capacity of the country was specious. The Peel Commission said:

"The heavy immigration in the years 1933-36 would seem to show that the Jews have been able to enlarge the absorptive capacity of the country for Jews."

The British response to Jewish immigration set a precedent of appeasing the Arabs, which was followed for the duration of the mandate. The British placed restrictions on Jewish immigration while allowing Arabs to enter the country freely. Arab populations were not considered when attempting to estimate the country's absorptive capacity. As persecution of Jews intensified in Europe during the Nazi era, the urgency driving the immigration became acute (41).

Figure 57: Zev, Rachel's future husband, is paving the roads in Israel with other chalozim (pioneers; 1936).

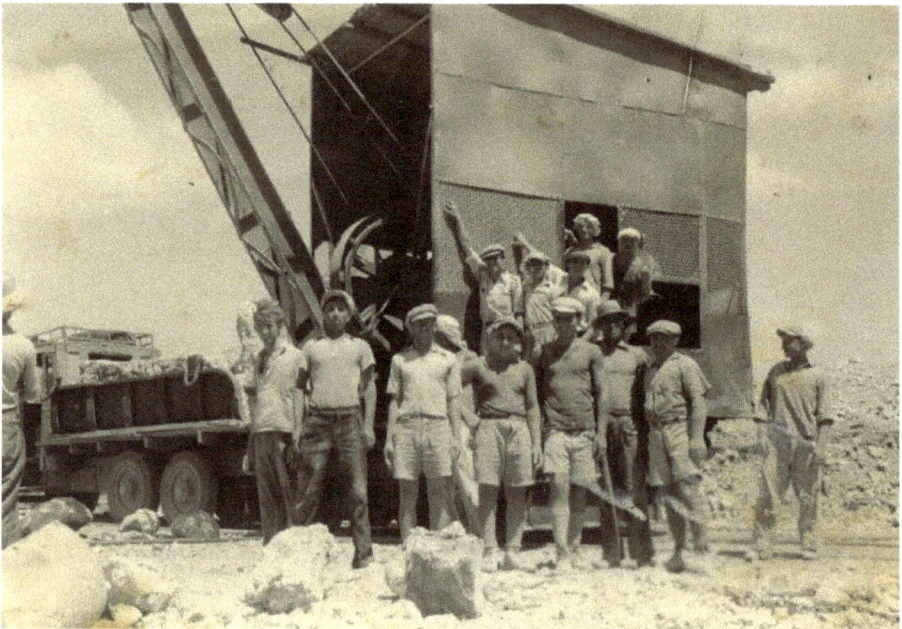

Figure 58: Zev paving the roads in Israel with other chalozim (1936).

Ha'apala (immigration to Israel) spread over 14 years from 1934-1948 when Israel achieved its independence, after which all Jews were welcome to their homeland. There were ups and downs during the operation and it was a difficult struggle against a huge empire who put heavy forces against the newcomers. The Jews had nothing left from their own home in Europe and wanted to live safely in a Jewish land. The Ha'apala was one of the most important projects of the Israeli nation in the first half of the 20th century (42).

During Ha'apala, few organizations composed of Jewish people in Europe and Israelis worked together to facilitate immigration beyond the established quotas. There were four components that constructed the successful operation by the Mossad LeAliyah Bet and several other organizations like Revisionists.

1. Most of the young people who volunteered to help in the operation were newcomers to Israel that participated in the youth groups and practiced living in Kibbutzim in Europe. They knew what would be ahead and were ready to do whatever would be needed to accomplish the goal.
2. The escorts: The pioneers who conquered the sea - they negotiated with the captains, instructed and supervised the captains and the ship's crew. They helped the pioneers embark the ship in Europe, accompanied the passengers from port to port, and helped them to disembark in Israel.
3. The operational group on the shore: on the Israeli beaches, volunteers and residents in the area cooperated as one unit to get the people off the ship. The residents in whatever area they landed, opened their doors to the newcomers and gave them hot showers, new clothes, and fed them until a place was organized for them.
4. The communication through the air, water, and land among different organizations in Israel and Europe: The telegraph/telephone connection from the Mossad LeAliyah Bet, that was a portion of the Haganah and was located in Tel Aviv, to the ships in the sea, informed the Mapilam of the exact movement of the English soldiers and their patrol ships. According to the incoming information the ships at sea would sail in the direction that would avoid the English and allow

them to land on a safe beach. This information worked in the opposite direction and enabled the people on the shore to be ready to welcome the Ma'apilim. In order to avoid the English patrol, the disembarkation happened only during the night. When the sun rose, the ships would sail back into the deep sea and come back the following night to let the remaining people reach the shore (43).

THE MAGNITUDE OF THE ALIYAH, TOLD BY SHAUL AVIGUR (HEAD OF MOSSAD ALIYAH)

"Like other historical projects, the first people who volunteered to be part of it did not estimate the complexity of the entire operation and the sources they needed to use in order to complete the mission. Only during the act itself, did the project get wings and they recognized that they were not walking on a side trail but they were paving a main road with their revolutionary function. They did not foresee that the Ha'apala would get to the dimensions it got. They only learned during the action itself how to proceed in spite of the obstacles, not give up, and find another way to get to their target. If it looked like they exhausted all the possibilities and all the abilities had vanished, they did not stop but continued to look for alternative ways. One door was closed, and a window had opened in the most unexpected place. The impossible became possible." (44, 45)

These are the people who helped Rachel. She could not get a certificate to enter Israel from the English government, and since she did not have anywhere else to go, she found alternate ways to reach her destination. She had to follow the path of illegal immigration.

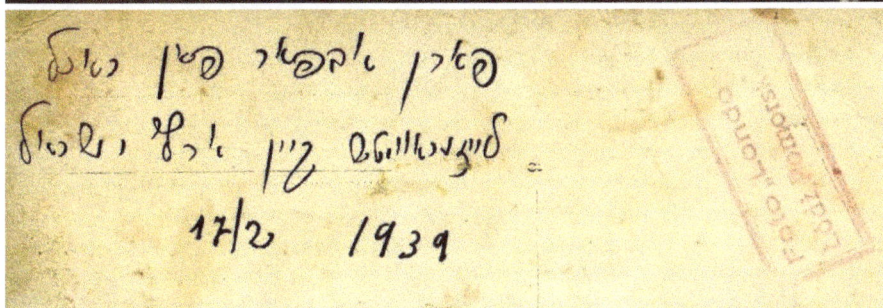

Figure 59: Rachel with her coworkers prior to leaving for Israel (February 17, 1939); Writing on the back of the picture (below).

THE VOYAGE TO ISRAEL

(FEBRUARY 28, 1939 TO APRIL 16, 1939)

PREPARING FOR THE VOYAGE

Rachel began her journey by boarding a train, which went through Lodz, Czechoslovakia, Hungary, and Romania and reached its destination in Constanta, a port city on the shore of the Black Sea. She waited on shore for a few days with the other passengers before boarding the ship. She made sure to send postcards and letters to her family to update them along her journey.

Jewish leadership was trying to bring as many Jews into Palestine as possible. They were purchasing old boats because of their limited budget, and then the boats were stripped to the bare bones in order to maximize the number of passengers. A ship named Jeepo B was docked in the port of Constanta waiting for the night. Rachel and the other passengers would eventually board the ship after eating a big meal.

The EZL (abbreviation in Hebrew from Irgun Zvai Leumi, a National Military Organization), purchased Jeepo B. It was a merchant ship with a volume of about 1,500 tons and flew a Panama flag. Prior to dealing with Israel, its major business was to transport ammunition from Sweden to Spain. Now its cargo was 750 immigrants from various youth groups in Europe.

This would be the second excursion of Jeepo to bring the Ma'apilim (ascending) to Israel. The first trip left the city on December 5, 1938 carrying 734 Jewish people from Austria, Romania, and Poland. In addition, it carried 100 Jews who came straight from the concentration camp Dachau, after the Gestapo agreed to let them go, only under one condition: that they would immediately leave the country. That first journey to Israel was smooth; all passengers arrived safely in Netanya. The ship came back to Constanta to make another trip and therefore got the name Jeepo B.

Early in February 1939, Itzhak Zarzevsky was invited to the EZL headquarters in Tel Aviv and was ordered to fly to the EZL office located in the Anglexi Hotel in Warsaw, Poland. Upon arrival, Itzhak was informed that he would be responsible for organizing the Jeepo B voyages, including loading items needed for the sail, boarding the people onto the ship, communicating with Israel about the departures and the routes, and coordinating the disembarkation of the passengers on the Israeli shore. Izchak oversaw the Jeepo B voyage from Bucharest in Romania and then to Constanta that was located on the shore of the Black Sea, south east of Romania where Rachel was waiting.

It was very difficult to buy and stock the ship with enough essential items to make it safely to Israel. Coal was needed for the engines, food and fresh water for the people, rescue boats for the voyage, and medication for Katina, a ship that was sailing to Israel with very sick people. The food products and coal could be bought only in small quantities and had to be stored in hidden places near the shore. They also needed to find boats with owners who would agree to move all the products onto the ship.

The operation was expensive and could only be done in the darkness of the night. Itzhak, who oversaw the operation, contacted the representative in Switzerland and asked him to transfer some money. The Swiss representative then communicated with a Greek friend who talked with the head of Perseus's secret police. With all their help, they were able to purchase food in quantities that would last for a few days until they were transferred to the troubled ship Katina.

Rachel waited patiently while hearing rumors that the trip could be delayed because the boat's owner and the staff were known pirates. They could surprise the Israeli leaders every step of the way with inflated expenses and squeeze money out of them by counting more people then were really on the boat. She could not do anything but wait.

She looked around and noticed an assertive person dressed in a suit walking among the passenger and looking for anyone with sailing experience. This man was Izchak. He selected from the passengers a few men who were trained as sailors in the Beitar. The Beitar was a Jewish youth movement. Once Izchak identified the skilled sailors among the passengers, he snuck them onto Jeepo B.

Later that day, Rachel saw the captain of the ship. He was from Greece and spoke some Russian. He was dressed like a pirate with a furry vest, a dagger attached to his belt, and high boots with spikes causing his footsteps to echo from a distance. He gave the impression of a wrestler going to a fight. Rumor had it that he was an experienced and fearless smuggler with whom no one wanted to mess with. This was the knight of the underground. Rachel saw Izchak and the man with high boots escorted by two people standing face-to-face arguing. She leaned closer to listen. It was like watching a show.

The Israeli had a steady voice when he told the captain that the last half of the payment would be paid when all passengers were boarded onto the ship. The captain laughed and demanded that if he would not get the money ahead of boarding, he would not take any of the passengers. The captain would command his sailors to weigh anchor and sail into the sea. To the captain's astonishment, Izchak calmly explained that there were already passengers on board with experience sailing who were ready to take over the ship and bring it to its destiny.

The captain became very angry and had no alternative but to calm down when Izchak refused to budge, looking straight at him, and waiting for agreement. As the argument continued, the captain realized that in this battle he had the lower hand and the more he spoke the worse it got.

Izchak advised the captain that if he would touch any of the Jewish representatives, the long hand of EZL would reach him for revenge. But if he would let the passenger go onto the ship respectfully, he would get paid as agreed. The captain reluctantly agreed. Rachel went back to her group of friends and shared with them her observation.

Figure 60: The Israelis stand up against the captain.

JEEPO B SETS SAIL

On February 28, 1939, the captain and the Israelis saw an approaching heavy cloud that would result in a dark night and gave the signal to start moving. The passengers, including Rachel, started to walk toward the ship. As they approached the ship, it got crowded but no one pushed.

Quickly and quietly, they climbed the ladder, one after the other. They were instructed ahead of time to bring only one bag or suitcase with them, not more.

Time was of the essence and a moment lost would hold back the sail. It was well controlled by the Beitar men on the ship. Rachel chose a mattress on the floor and put her bag on the ship's wall adjacent to it, to claim her space. After all the passengers embarked onto the ship, the food was loaded; it included a huge amount of regular and toasted bread, canned meat, fruit, and vegetables. The sacks and boxes were loaded in a few hours. At sunrise, the ship sailed to the sea.

At sunset, the ship stopped and Rachel, with others on the deck, spotted a motorboat far away that was slowly getting close to them. When it reached the side of the ship, she saw ropes thrown down to the motorboat, and a few boxes were tied carefully with the ropes and hoisted up into the ship. They looked like the other food boxes, but she found later that they held ammunition for the EZL to use in Israel.

The sea was angry, and the waves were high. Since it was her first time on a ship, Rachel was not used to the movement of the waves and tried to avoid throwing up by spending most of the time on the deck. The ship progressed slowly.

During the next few days, they sailed while storms with strong winds and high waves crashed against the ship. The ship stopped in Corinth Bay. The Israeli leader informed them that one of the London newspapers had misleading news that an illegal ship, which left Constanta while Jeepo B left that port, was devoured at sea with all its passengers. He gave each of the 750 passengers a mailing card, so they could write to their families in Europe that they are alive. An order was given not to mention their current location, their destination, or the expected time of arrival to Israel. All nodded their head yes to the request. However, in a close inspection of the cards, prior to mailing, the leaders found a postcard with all forbidden details addressed to relatives in Israel. This was a lesson that every operation requires key checkpoints in the execution, up to the smallest detail, to ensure security of the project.

On March 4, 1939 Jeepo B met Katina in Kalamakia, near the gulf of Corinth, in the island of Alonissos. They transferred food, medications,

and some rescue boats to Katina. The Israeli leaders agreed that Katina would sail immediately to Israel. Jeepo B would wait in the port for two more days.

Figure 61: The Ma'apilim boarding Jeepo B.

Katina sailed to Israel on March 7, stopping in ports of Turkey and Greece to fill up with freshwater. Katina made long diversions to hide from the English air patrol. Airplanes were constantly circling above Katina, and the stops at different ports did not help to conceal the ship. Their captain put up a black flag to make it look like a plague was on board.

JEEPO B SINKS NEAR CRETE (MARCH 10, 1939)

On March 9th, as agreed, Jeepo B left Kalamakia port and sailed at full steam. Everything was going smoothly; Rachel and the others were very happy that they were sailing at last, the commander had no complaints, and the ship was stocked with food and water. When people were content with the food, they were more comfortable following instructions. They all truly believed that they would reach the shores of Israel soon and the commanders would come back to Constanta with the ship to get another round of passengers.

The night was clear, the moon was full, and the sea was quiet as the people slept peacefully. Rachel snuck onto the deck and watched the shore of Greece fade into the distance. Once she could no longer see land, she slipped back down to her mattress and settled below deck.

Suddenly, a huge noise cut through the silence of the night, almost like a huge clap of thunder rolling across the deck. The shaking of the ship made it seem as though it had hit something. Another huge boom rang through the silence, and the ship stopped moving altogether. Rachel was thrown from her mattress and woke up to widespread chaos. Still trying to discern what had happened, she heard a terrible noise from the ship's belly moments before it began rocking side-to-side. The first people on the deck were the commanders with Rachel following closely behind. The chief engineer screamed: "Every man for himself!" Rachel sitting curled up like a fearful child, asked herself what should she do? She did not move, she just sat and waited.

Three miles from the beach, the ship had run aground on a colossal rock near the southern island Crete in the Mediterranean Sea. It was still three miles from the shore. Rachel heard the instruction and hurried below deck, where she saw the Israeli leaders trying to stem the flow of panic that was spreading through the passengers. The word around the ship was that they needed to get at least 200 people off to lighten the weight. The people had to throw all their belongings into the sea while evacuating the boat. Rachel did as she was told but kept the one important thing she had from home, the silver kiddush cup that her father used while blessing the wine. She hid it in her bra and carried it to safety.

The decision was made that women and children would leave first. Rachel climbed the stairs back to the deck while the crew did their best to control the crowd of people fighting to make their way into a line. At the bottom of the ship, there were two openings where water was rushing in. These holes were guarded by crew members who did not want the passengers to know the truth: the situation was helpless; the ship was going down. While Rachel went to the deck, she saw that the Israeli leaders had gathered people to play cards, effectively easing the panic that was threatening to consume the ship. However, another problem was at hand. It seemed that the remaining rescue boats had holes in them and were unfit for passengers.

The ship's siren screeched with what little life it had left. As flares were shot into the sky, all the noises showed Rachel that whatever could be done to save them was being done. The telegraph was repeating its S.O.S. call for anyone who was able to receive it.

Rachel was on the deck waiting amongst other scared women when she spotted it: a fisherman's vessel coming nearer and nearer. The Israeli leaders began to talk with the fishermen about moving people ashore, but the conversation soon became a negotiation over price. The fishermen wanted to be paid in a foreign currency, and they asked for a large sum. After agreeing, Rachel and about fifty others were lowered into the fishing vessel and were taken ashore.

Later Rachel learned the crowd aboard Jeepo B pushed and shoved as they tried to force their way onto the upper deck. They were allowed to go up to the deck in groups of ten, while the rest waited anxiously below deck. Some passengers were drafted to bail the steady flow of water out using the ship's pumps. However, they quickly realized that their task was pointless; for every gallon of water they got out, two more gallons entered.

On the boat a heavy rope was dangling from the flagpole with numbered circles. The circle number 175 had already touched the water. It took two hours from the time the ship struck the rock to the time it sunk thirty circles, about two meters. With a quick calculation the sailors realized that within six hours the water would reach the deckhand and cover the ship completely.

Each of the fisherman's trips took an hour, meaning that 300 people would be saved in the best scenario. As the sun rose, they all wondered if their siren was heard, if the S.O.S. reach someone, and if help would arrive in time to save more people.

Figure 62: Sunrise, photographed by Erez Liebermann, Rachel's Grandson (August 2020).

Towing Ship to the Rescue (March 11, 1939)

After being taken ashore by the fisherman's boat, Rachel was sitting quietly on the island on a bare rock with the other 200 survivors. She did not know what would happen, and the only thing to do was to watch the sea.

Figure 63: Rachel sitting on a rock in Crete waiting for her rescue.

Suddenly, she saw that people were pointing toward a dot on the horizon that grew larger and larger. Shouts of happiness burst from the people's mouths. As it got closer, they saw a towing ship that had repair machines on its deck. The rescue mechanics tried to put automatic pumps in Jeepo B. One of the pumps fell into the water, and the rest pumped the water with no success. The captain consulted with his crew and the Israeli leaders and decided to abandon the ship completely.

Figure 64: Jeepo B passengers moving to Katina.

Then the group on shore realized that another approaching ship was a familiar ship, Katina. Upon receiving Jeepo B's S.O.S., Katina immediately turned around. They were saved. They watched as passengers from the half sunk Jeepo B were transferred to Katina and knew that their turn would come soon. As expected, some small boats came to rescue Rachel and the other 200 passengers patiently waiting on shore.

After all the people from Jeepo B were rescued, they targeted whatever supplies they could salvage and use on Katina. A group of people from Katina went back into the Jeepo B despite the captain's protest as they could lose their life returning to a sinking ship. They took as much as they could from Jeepo B onto the rescue boats. On the last trip, the ship sank, sadly taking two sailors down with it.

When the captain on Katina was instructed to pick up the survivors from Jeepo B, the people on board objected since there were already 800 people trying to survive on the old fragile boat. By sundown, Rachel and the rest were situated on Katina. It was very different from Jeepo B. Katina floated for the past weeks with little food and rampant disease and now they had to take on more people totaling 1,550 people on board. Much more than the boat was built to carry.

Katina was now over the maximum capacity, but no one saw any other option. There was not enough food or room for mattresses. Sick people were all over throwing up. People were fighting for no reason; the boat was dirty and lice infested. There was hunger. People cooked whatever they had for themselves without sharing. Those who got sick and died were thrown overboard. Rachel, touching the kiddush cup frequently to ensure its presence, prayed to God asking for a safe trip.

Katina traveled to the nearest port. The Israeli leaders decided that one of them would leave the ship and make his way to Israel to get advice and re-plan the voyage of the two ships combined to one.

Katina stayed at the port for two more days. On the third day, Katina's captain announced that they could not get closer to Israel's shore because the ship would be recognized by the British patrol and their agents, who were scattered all over the Mediterranean Sea watching for illegal ships in every port. The Israeli leaders, after consultation, decided to repaint the boat and change the name to "Andikala," so it was unrecognizable.

Rachel became closely acquainted with the people around her seated on the crowded upper deck. Soon the deck became even more constrained with the rush of people from the lower deck. A happy energy radiated and Rachel soon found that food was coming. At midday Rachel saw a fishing boat approaching the ship. It was loaded with bags of bread, rice, vegetables, and canned goods that were the supplies to last for a week until Katina reached its destination. During the darkness of the night, Katina finally set sail again.

Figure 66: 1939 – A map of Rachel's trip to Israel.

The ship glided smoothly on the water to its destination. Rachel was sitting in her spot when suddenly she saw the shore lines of Israel. She felt as if a joyful blanket had come down from above to cover and protect her. In a few hours, she would be able to reach the Promised Land and see her brother.

הערות	גורם המארגן	מספר המעפילים	מקום ההגעה	נמל ההפלגה	תאריך ההגעה	תאריך ההפלגה	שם האניה
	ההסתדרות דהחלוץ	350	כפר ויתקין נתניה תל-אביב	פירואוס	יולי 34		1 וילוס א'
17 נתפסו ונדרשו סרסורי.	בית"ר	117	תל-אביב		אוגוסט 34		2 אונטון
50 הצליחו לרדת בזמן ויתקין ואו נתגלתה על-ידי משטר החוזים הבריטי ונלכד לעזה. שוטטה במשך עשרה שבועות בים התיכון ולבסוף החזירה את המעפילים לאירופה.	החלוץ דהחלוציה	350	כפר ויתקין	ווינה	ספטמבר 34		3 וילוס ב'
	מ' עליה ובית"ר	15	חיפה		11.4.37		4 אר'על'פי
	מ' עליה ובית"ר	54	שונטורה	אלבניה	ספטמבר 37		5 אר'על'פי
	המוסד לעליה	65	אביהיל	פיראוס	12.1.38	3.1.38	6 פוסידון א'
	מ' עליה ובית"ר	96			מארס 38		7 אר'על'פי
	המוסד לעליה	128		פיראוס	13.4.38	10.4.38	8 ארטמיזיה א'
	המוסד לעליה	65		פיראוס	13.5.38	17.5.38	9 פוסידון ב'
							10 אר'על'פי
	מ' עליה ובית"ר	141		פיראוס	38 יוני		11 אר'על'פי
							12 אר'על'פי
	המוסד לעליה	157		פיראוס	13.7.38	16.7.38	13 ארטמיזיה ב'
	בית"ר	140	שטורה	סידון	אוקטובר 38		14 דראגא א'
	המוסד לעליה	300		באר	20.11.38	25.11.38	15 אסטיר א'
	ביתר	550	נתניה	קונסטנצה	דצמבר 38	סוף נוב 38	16 דראגא ב'
	בית"ר	540		קונסטנצה	דצמבר 38	סוף נוב 38	17 אלי
	בית"ר	734		קונסטנצה		5.12.38	18 ניסא א'
	בית"ר	250		קונסטנצה	דצמבר 1938		19 דלפה
	המוסד לעליה	300		מוקולה	15.1.39	9.1.39	20 אסטיר ב'
225 מעפילים הצליחו לרדת ב-6.2.39 באניית 'ארטמיזיה'. בחוף הרצליה ואז נתפסה האניה והוחלפה. 'קאמינינו' הועידה במשך שבועיים בים התיכון. עם מעט סיון וחמצן רצוף. ולבסוף הצליחו לקבל עזר 750 מעפילים נוספים מן האניה 'ניסא' שטבעה בסמוכת שנעיה ליד פיראוס. הצליחו להוריד 600 מעפילים נוספים. חזרו ליון והחזירו בחזרה. שבועו לאחר פסח הורדו הצליחו להוריד 350 מעפילים נבא ויתקין. יתר המעפילים (375) הפני במרים להיעצם יחד עם 'אסיטי' ולאחר הגעת הספינים הבריטים להורידם החר.	בית"ר	600	הרצליה	קונסטנצה	6.2.39	ינואר 39	21 קאמינינו
	המוסד לעליה	300		נאפולי	20.2.39	15.2.39	22 אסטרטו ג'
	המוסד לעליה	376		סוזק	13.3.39	7.3.39	23 אסרטו ד'
	ברזי	270			22.3.39		24 סנדו
סוזעד ב-8.4.39 לאבנהיל ומחמת היום הטובי הורדו 92 מעפילים בלבד. נעצרו שני דיים הורו עוד 100 מעפילים ליד קיסריה ואז נתפסה הספינה והובבד לחיפה. ב-13.4.39 נורדה לפני ים שעות לקוששטנצה. ב-64.3.39 לקוטנית נתפסה. מפאלו ט20 מפוסה הקורבן 'נימס'.	גילוים כלליי	470	אבידחיל	קונסטנצה	8.4.39	1.4.39	25 אסטימי
סוזעד ליד ברזין ב-25 במארס 1939. מעפילים 1939. נעבורו לספינות 'קאמינו' והרצו באמרד אדצה. 1939	בית"ר	750		קונסטנצה		1.3.1939	26 נימס ב'
		400			22.4.39		27 ניסא רוני

Figure 67: 1939 - Documentation of the history of Jeepo B and Katina (46).

RACHEL'S ARRIVAL IN NETANYA (APRIL 16, 1930)

The disembarkation was scheduled to take place in the darkness of the night. In the morning, Rachel and the rest were woken early and informed to eat quickly and stay in the breakfast area. Everyone was seated quietly, anxious to hear the instructions for the upcoming night. The Israeli leaders entered the room and silence fell over the crowd.

One of them gave a cheerful speech, "Brothers and sisters, today will be a memorable day. Today you will be walking on the ground of the holy land. Our trip was longer than expected, full of brick walls that we doubted we would overcome. But we did it. Unfortunately, we had casualties that did not make it to this moment, but these hardships along the way are common in Jewish history. Getting over them is what unites us with the rest of the Jews and makes us stronger.

Now the world is against us and countries have kicked us out or have not accepted us, but you have finally reached your home land, the land where our ancestors grew up. Here you will be free and independent. Please consider your suffering as a sacrifice to allow you to reach your main goal: landing in the desired land. Today you have witnessed that there are no obstacles preventing us from returning to our home land. Hooray to the free country, Israel!"

Figure 68: Sunrise over Masada, photographed by Oren Liebermann, Rachel's grandson, 2011.

Rachel touched the kiddush cup and prayed to God, "Thank you Adonai Eloaino Adonai Echad for bringing me to this water and this land. I know that I will be free in the land of my ancestors and can practice my religion and study whatever I want."

Within a minute, she joined everyone else in joyful and loud singing and dancing. This was the first time that there was so much happiness on this ship. She looked around at her fellow passengers and realized that all the misery, tiredness, and sickness that overcame them earlier had disappeared and now their eyes sparkled with joy.

The instructions were clear: By midday everyone was to shower and dress with clean clothes. From noon until night, no one was allowed to be on the upper deck. After lunch, each passenger would stand by their backpack. All the certificates, passports, and any other identifying papers had to be thrown into the sea. The entire ship had to be silent and everyone had to sit with their own group and wait patiently to disembark.

At midnight, six miles from the shore of Netanya, the ship threw an anchor. Rachel, who was sitting on the upper deck, saw that the two Beitar men went into a small boat and rowed with their utmost power. The boat flipped when they were midway, and they fell into the water. They did not waste time, they continued to swim to shore.

They found a big group of people waiting for them. That group learned in advance the estimated arrival time of Katina and were ready on shore to move the Ma'apilim off the ship. They heard about the diseases that spread among the people on the ship and had brought medical equipment, nurses, and doctors to supply first aid. The amount of people who came to assist with disembarking was double than usual because of the number of passengers on board and the limited time they had until daylight.

Figure 69: Rachel being rescued in Netanya beach.

Meanwhile on the boat, Rachel was watching the shore very carefully, and she spotted a light signaling the ship. Immediately after, the ship approached the shore. One of the Beitar men swam back to the ship, and the disembarkation began. The rescue boats were lowered to the water in a specific order. First were sick people, then women, then children, and lastly the older men. It was going smoothly; the boats were coming and going, and the Beitar group was controlling the situation perfectly on the boat (47).

Rachel waited for her turn. She had nothing to carry with her but the hidden kiddush cup. She climbed quickly down the ladder and sat in the boat. Once it was filled with people, they rowed the boat as quickly as they could. As they approached the shore, they had to jump into the shallow waters and swim or wade to dry land while holding a rope connecting Katina to the shore.

She searched for her brother, but she could not find him. Later, she learned that her brother, Joseph Lajzerowicz, who lived in Israel, was expecting her. For three nights, he waited on the shore with the rescue squad, but she never arrived. Each night, he was so disappointed that he burst into tears. He cried so loudly that his friends kept the possibility of the ship arriving on the fourth night a secret, because they did not want him to gain hope just to be disappointed again.

The newcomers were directed to the warehouse where Israelis residents would sort and box oranges for shipping. The rescue team on the shore gave the immigrants khaki clothes so they could mingle with the Israeli workers who were on their way to the orchard. The reason for this action plan was to make it so that English patrol would not know the difference between a native Israeli and a newcomer. There was a strict order for the newcomers not to say anything so the British soldiers would not be able to detect their accent.

Rachel was desperate to know where her brother was, but an Israeli soldier shepherding the immigrants to the warehouse pointed a pistol at her head and said, "You need to be quiet. If you talk, the English will detect your different accent and arrest all of us." Then, under the fear of the British patrol, Rachel fell silent.

Rachel stayed in the warehouse until the morning, when the orchard gates were opened, and people began their work. Rachel went to one of the workers and asked him where she was. When the answer was Netanya, she could not believe it and asked a few others just to be sure. They knew her brother Joseph and offered to take her to his house, but Rachel did not trust them.

She ran and ran, asking people for directions to her brother's location. She ran through the sands of Netanya. She had no luggage and no shoes on her feet, only her underwear and her dress. As she had done before, from time to time, she touched the kiddush cup, prayed, and asked God to safely lead her to her brother.

Figure 71: Rachel running to her brother in Netanya.

Rachel finally reached his house, but only the landlord was there to welcome her. She looked at Rachel and forbade her from entering the house because she was so dirty. The landlord took Rachel's dress and underwear and burned them in the backyard while Rachel bathed in an aluminum bathtub in the garden. The landlord scrubbed her with a rough brush, using disinfectant to kill the lice, and cleaning her off with running water from a garden hose. Wearing clothes that the landlord gave her, Rachel was allowed to enter the house where she ate a good breakfast and slept for a full day and night.

Figure 72: The landlord washing Rachel in the backyard.

Figure 73: A disinfectant pump used to get rid of lice.

She woke up for a short time to see Joseph and her sister-in-law, Pnina, bending over her bed checking if she was alive. Rachel showed them the kiddush cup that she carried from her home in Poland, over countries and seas to Israel. Then they all celebrated her arrival in Israel.

Figure 74: Joseph and Pnina welcoming Rachel to the Promised Land.

Later, after World War II ended, Rachel found out that the German regime killed her parents and five brothers and sisters in the concentration camps. She became rooted in Israel. She learned the Hebrew language, found a job, met her husband, got married, and gave birth to my brother Uri and me.

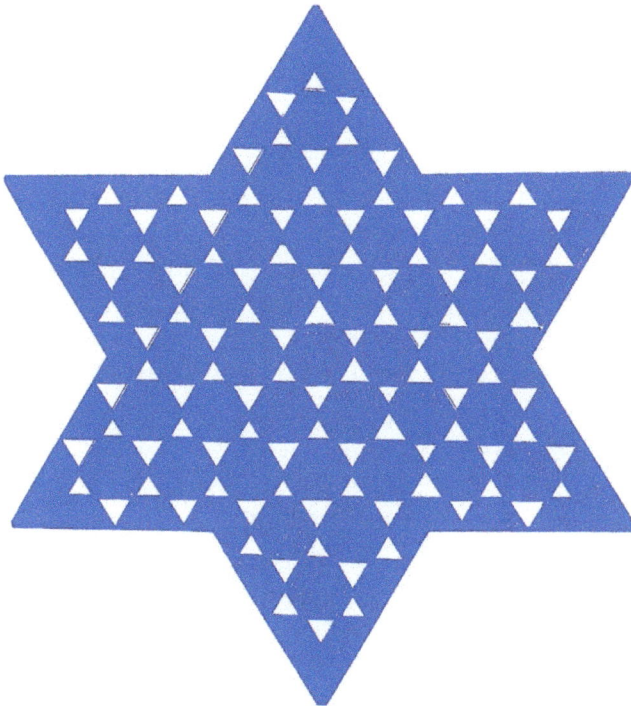

Figure 75: Star of David created by Tamar, Rachel's granddaughter, 1980.

REFLECTIONS

My mother kept the most important thing she had from back home, the silver kiddush cup, throughout her entire journey. To her dying day, when I asked her to tell the story of her Aliyah to me and her grandchildren, she pulled her shirt slightly away from her chest with her left hand and imitated putting the cup into her bra with her right hand. She had nightmares, but never talked about them. During my childhood, when I entered the house from the garden or feeding our turkeys and tried to clean my fingernails using the opposite nails, my mother used to ask me to stop. The act reminded her of the way they would get rid of lice while on the ship.

I wrote a short version of this story 20 years ago, and I began to write this longer version at the beginning of the pandemic of COVID-19 in February 2020. I wanted to document the story of my mother, her life in Poland, why she was forced to leave, and how difficult the Aaliyah was for her. I read many documents about Jews in Poland, the Ma'apilim subject, and especially the two ships, Jeepo B and Katina. Finally, I understood how my mother was fighting for her life and strived to survive. She had a strong sense of what steps needed to be taken to get to the Promised Land.

The conclusion is simple: we must look out for ourselves first. People can advise and instruct us how to live our life, but in the end, it is up to each of us to choose the next step: look around, assess the situation, and act accordingly.

At the completion of her story, I realized what made my mother successful: she did not make a big deal out of little obstacles. She appreciated life in a positive light and did not question the purpose of her existence. She suffered from rheumatoid arthritis when she got older but never complained and went through her day managing the regular activities of a housewife. Strangely, after ten years, the disease vanished. She simply let irritating issues slide by. After feeling death closely approaching and then escaping it, she adapted the right attitude towards life.

Why do we need a life-threatening situation to recognize and treasure the gifts that we receive from God? My mother died on August 3, 1999 in Haifa. I hope that her memories and experiences live forever through this book and inspire other people to follow their heart. She was a wonderful mother, and I hope I was a good daughter.

ACKNOWLEDGMENTS

I would like to thank my husband, Eli, who supported me in the long process of creating this story. I would like to thank Katie Soko, the artist that illustrated the beautiful figures and prepared the book for publishing. I would like to thank all my family and friends who helped me with various subjects along the way. Thanks to my grandson, Michael Zev Liebermann, who helped me to write a chapter in the story. Thanks to my granddaughters, Kaila Ann Brooks and Rachel Delores Brooks, and my daughter, Tamar Liebermann Brooks, MSE, MBA, photographer, who edited my story to make it more appealing.

Figure 76: Rachel with her son, Uri, holding the kiddush cup.

ABOUT THE AUTHOR:

Yaffa Liebermann
Physical Therapist, APTA Geriatric Certified Specialist

Figure 77: My mother Rachel and me in 1986.

Yaffa Liebermann was born in Kfar-Ata, Israel in 1945. The family lived in a simple wooden structure that was part of a chain of apartments. Each home consisted of an entrance hall/dining room, a kitchen and a great room. All together the place was only about 600 square feet (60 square meters). The toilet and showers were outside the apartment in another stretch of wooden housing. Yaffa had a good childhood, played with friends and read stories with her mother while sitting on a bench in front of the house. Her parents worked very hard and they moved to a house when Yaffa was 8 years old.

She became a Physical Therapist and served in the Israel Defense Forces during the 1967 war, where she gained experience treating war-related injuries from both sides of the fence. It was painful for her to learn how devastating a war could be. She met her husband while serving in the army, after he sustained an injury rolling down a hill in his home town, and required physical therapy.

Yaffa worked in a variety of settings: hospitals, out-patients, psychiatric facilities, home care rehabilitation for spinal cord, and brain trauma in Israel, Switzerland, and the U.S.A. (Virginia and New Jersey).

She found her love and passion while working with the elderly in the nursing home environment in New Jersey. Yaffa became a Geriatric Certified Specialist (GCS), board certified by the American Physical Therapy Association (APTA) in 1998.

In 1996, Yaffa founded Prime Rehabilitation Services, Inc, along with her husband and her daughter Tamar, with the goal of providing the highest quality rehabilitation services to sub-acute nursing home facilities throughout New Jersey, New York, and Pennsylvania.

From working in the field, she saw the need to author four books. Her first book was focused on care for a stroke patient, instructing caregivers on the proper care of patients in the first few days after the stroke and continued home care. Three more books were about correct children's posture, with the hope that they will learn how to stand up straight at a young age and carry their bodies with pride.

Yaffa has been married for more than 53 years to a wonderful husband who always supports her wishes. They have four children and eight grandchildren. Yaffa continues to work and enjoys traveling.

Yaffa Liebermann's books available online:

- Stroke Restoration - Functional Movement for Patients and Caregivers - 2008

- I Stand Up Straight Poem and Exercises - 2010

- Rachel, Pedro and Friends Stand Up Straight. An Activity book - 2014

- Rachel, Pedro and Friends Sit Up Straight. An Activity book - 2014

ABOUT THE ILLUSTRATOR:

Katie Sokolowski, PhD, DABT

Katie Sokolowski is a diplomate of the American Board of Toxicologists and received her doctorate in neurotoxicology from the Joint Graduate Program in Toxicology at Rutgers University. At heart, Katie is a naturalist obsessed with understanding the natural world of biology. Her obsessions propelled her professional career in neurotoxicology while remaining active in her artwork.

She has been illustrating for Yaffa Liebermann for over 20 years. Throughout Katie's education, from high school right through post-doctoral training and right up until her current position, Yaffa consistently had a new project for them to collaborate on. This book holds a special place on her shelf because it was one of the first collaborations they started. A good story needs time to develop.

REFERENCES

1. Zduńska Wola - Wikipedia ; en.wikipedia.org › wiki › Zduńska_Wola.

2. Rosenberg, Phillip. "City of My Birth, Reminiscences of Zdunska-Wola." Zduńska-Wola, Poland (English Pages 3-30) - JewishGen: www.jewishgen.org › yizkor › Zdunska_Wola › zdue003 (page 23-29).

3. Goldberg, Jacob. "The History of Jewish Settlement in Zdunska-Wola." Zduńska-Wola, Poland (English Pages 3-30) - JewishGen: www.jewishgen.org › yizkor › Zdunska_Wola › zdue00 (page 6).

4. "Zdunska Wola" - Encyclopedia of Jewish, Communities in Poland, Volume I (Poland) 51°36' / 18°56' Translation of "Zdunska Wola." chapter from *Pinkas Hakehillot Polin*, published by Yad Vashem.

5. Ehrlich Elchanan: The History of the Zduńska Wola Jews by Dr. Yakov Goldberg: The Zduńska Wola Book. Edited by Leila Kaye-Klin, Published in Tel Aviv, April 1968.

6. rabbi | Definition, History, & Functions | Britannica, www.britannica.com › ... › Religious Beliefs Rabbi, Judaism, Written By: The Editors of Encyclopaedia Britannica.

7. Images for Spinning Wheel and Weaving Loom Diagrams.

8. Spinning Wheel and Weaving Loom Diagrams - Apple Hollow … www.applehollow.com › ahf-ueparts.

9. How a Spinning Wheel Spins Yarn – Dreaming Robots; www.dreamingrobots.com › Spinning.

10. http://www.allfiberarts.com/library/aa00/aa030800.htm.

11. Spin-Off, Spring 2003 Digital Edition – Long Thread Media; shop.longthreadmedia.com › products › spin-off-spring.

12. *Milk*: Why milk is so good for you? http://www.moomilk.com/faq.htm.

13. Milk Homogenization - HORIBA; www.horiba.com › particle-characterization › application.

14. Ingredients for Cheese Making at Home | Cheese Making; cheesemaking.com › blogs › learn › ingredients-for-ch.

15. How to Make Fromage Blanc (Cultured Soft Cheese): practicalselfreliance.com › Cheesemaking.

16. The Cheese Library. Basic Cheese making. http://cheesenet.wgx.com/cheesent/library.asp?action=read&ID=3.

17. *https://www.maureenabood.com/homemade-butter-you-have-to/.*

18. The Old Fashioned Way: Homemade Butter Recipe - Tori Avey; toriavey.com › ... › Passover › Passover - Ashkenaz.

19. http://www.hertzmann.com/articles/2001/fromage/.

20. https://www.chabad.org/library/article_cdo/aid/133896/jewish/Waiting-Periods-Between-Meat-Dairy.ht.

21. *Jewish cooking, eating habits and holiday and sabbath food;* factsanddetails.com › world › cat55 › sub396 › item1363.

22. Shabbat Blessings for Friday Night | My Jewish Learning; www.myjewishlearning.com › article › shabbat-blessings.

23. Otiker Israel: "About the book." The Hachalotz movement in Poland. Its growth and Development; 1932-1935. page 8-10. Beit Lochamei Haghettaot- Ghetto Fighters' House Kibbutz Hamaeuchad Publishing House Ltd., 1972.

24. Aliyah - Wikipedia; en.wikipedia.org › wiki › Aliyah.

25. The world of the Jewish youth movement – infed.org: by Daniel Rose.

26. Otiker Israel: "General rules in the development of the HaChalotz movement." The Hachalotz movement in Poland. Its growth and Development; 1932-1935. pages 63- 68. Beit Lochamei Haghettaot- Ghetto Fighters' House Kibbutz Hamaeuchad Publishing House Ltd., 1972.

27. Dobnov Shimon, Polin Kingdom. Hate in Poland. The History Of the Eternal Nation. ("Devray Yamay Am Olam") First book, 4th chapter: page 122, The Dvir Co. Tel Aviv, Israel. 1958.

28. Blood Libel | The Holocaust Encyclopedia: encyclopedia.ushmm.org › content › article › blood-libel.

29. Blood libel - Wikipediaen.wikipedia.org › wiki › Blood_libel.

30. Jewish poll tax - Wikipedia: en.wikipedia.org › wiki › Jewish_poll_ta.

31. Jewish Clothing | My Jewish Learning: www.myjewishlearning.com › article › jewish-clothing.

32. Schwartz Madeleine *E.M.* Rose reconsiders where the anti-Semitic slur came from, and how it stuck around..The Origins of Blood Libel | The Nation; www.thenation.com › article › archive › Jan 28, 2016.

33. The Polish Bakery: A Glorious Institution | Article | Culture.pl; culture.pl › article; the-polish-bakery-a-glorious-instit.

34. Tailoring - Jewish Virtual Library : www.jewishvirtuallibrary.org › tailoring.

35. Lodz Poland Jewish history tour, Jewish virtual library. https://www.jewishvirtuallibrary.org/lodz-poland-jewish-history.

36. Otiker Israel. "The Human subject in the HaChalotz. The details of the members in the branches: the ages, sex, seniority, and education in the youth movement." The Hachalotz movement in Poland. Its growth and Development; 1932-1935. pages 52-55. Beit Lochamei Haghettaot- Ghetto Fighters' House Kibbutz Hamaeuchad Publishing House Ltd., 1972.

37. https://www.history.com/topics/holocaust/kristallnacht

38. Balfour Declaration - Wikipedia, en.wikipedia.org › wiki › Balfour_Declaration.

39. British Restrictions on Jewish Immigration to Palestine www.jewishvirtuallibrary.org › british-restrictions-on-je.

40. Mandate For Palestine - The Legal Aspects of Jewish Rights; www.mythsandfacts.org › conflict › mandate_for_pales.

41. Peel Commission - Wikipedia; en.wikipedia.org › wiki › Peel Commission; *Palestine Royal Commission Report* (the Peel Report), (London: 1937), page 300.

42. The Struggle against Jewish Immigration to Palestine - jstor: www.jstor.org › stable.

43. Naor, Mordechai. "The Organization for Aliyah B," The Immigration ('Hapala") 1934-1948. Publisher Ministry of Defence. TelAviv Israel. 1988; pages 40-41.

44. Naor, Mordechai. "A Summary of an Historical undertaking." The Immigration ("Hapala") 1934-1948. Publisher Ministry of Defence. TelAviv Israel. 1988; page 133.

45. Ha'Mossad Le'Aliya Bet; www.palyam.org › English › HaMossad › main page.

46. Col. Wallach, Jehuda. Carta's Atlas of Palestine From Zionism To Statehood. Carta, Jerusalem, Israel 1974.

47. Avneri Arieh L. "Jepo B," "This is how Jeepo B demented at the sea," Velos to Taurus: The first decade of Jewish 'illegal' immigration to Mandatory Palestine (ErezIsrael) 1934-1944: pages 99-111.

www.ingramcontent.com/pod-product-compliance
Lightning Source LLC
Chambersburg PA
CBHW040254100426
42811CB00011B/1259